SENIORS ON STAGE

SENIORS ON STAGE

The Impact of Applied Theatre Techniques on the Elderly

Patch Clark
and
Nancy J. Osgood

PRAEGER

PRAEGER SPECIAL STUDIES • PRAEGER SCIENTIFIC

New York • Philadelphia • Eastbourne, UK
Toronto • Hong Kong • Tokyo • Sydney

Library of Congress Cataloging in Publication Data

Clark, Patch.
  Seniors on stage.

  Bibliography: p.
  Includes index.
  1. Theater and the aged.   2. Aged—Recreation.
  3. Aging in literature.   4. Drama in education.
  I. Osgood, Nancy J.   II. Title.
  PN3160.A34C55   1985   792'.088056   85-9347
  ISBN 0-03-069553-8 (alk. paper)

Published and Distributed by the
Praeger Publishers Division
(ISBN Prefix 0-275)
of Greenwood Press, Inc.,
Westport, Connecticut

Published in 1985 by Praeger Publishers
CBS Educational and Professional Publishing, a Division of CBS Inc.
521 Fifth Avenue, New York, NY 10175 USA

© 1985 by Praeger Publishers

All rights reserved

56789 052 987654321

Printed in the United States of America on acid-free paper

INTERNATIONAL OFFICES

Orders from outside the United States should be sent to the appropriate address listed below. Orders from areas not listed below should be placed through CBS International Publishing, 383 Madison Ave., New York, NY 10175 USA

Australia, New Zealand
Holt Saunders, Pty, Ltd., 9 Waltham St., Artarmon, N.S.W. 2064, Sydney, Australia

Canada
Holt, Rinehart & Winston of Canada, 55 Horner Ave., Toronto, Ontario, Canada M8Z 4X6

Europe, the Middle East, & Africa
Holt Saunders, Ltd., 1 St. Anne's Road, Eastbourne, East Sussex, England BN21 3UN

Japan
Holt Saunders, Ltd., Ichibancho Central Building, 22-1 Ichibancho, 3rd Floor, Chiyodaku, Tokyo, Japan

Hong Kong, Southeast Asia
Holt Saunders Asia, Ltd., 10 Fl, Intercontinental Plaza, 94 Granville Road, Tsim Sha Tsui East, Kowloon, Hong Kong

Manuscript submissions should be sent to the Editorial Director, Praeger Publishers, 521 Fifth Avenue, New York, NY 10175 USA

This book is warmly dedicated to
the memory of my grandparents
and all grandparents,
past, present, and future

P.C.

ACKNOWLEDGMENTS

The authors would like to thank all those who made the completion of this book possible. First, our thanks to all the senior adults and site directors who graciously opened their doors and hearts to us. We would like to thank Angelyn Poe and Linda Harden, who conducted drama programs at the Richmond sites. We would like to thank the Faculty Grants-In-Aid Program at Virginia Commonwealth University for making our research possible. We would also like to express our appreciation to Dr. Stan Orchowsky for his assistance in the program, Diane Sadler Martin for her support during the writing of this book, and Jerry Crabb for his hopeful outlook.

Finally, we would like to thank our families, Ray Jordan, Cressida Osgood, Ron, and Rob Clark for their continued support throughout the project.

The authors gratefully acknowledge permission to use the following material:
Emma, by Wendy Kesselman, adapted and reprinted by permission of Joan Daves. Doubleday & Company, Inc., 1980. Text copyright©1980 by Wendy Kesselman.
On Golden Pond by E. Thompson, published by Dodd, Mead & Company, 1979. Copyright©1979 by Ernest Thompson. Reprinted by permission of Dodd, Mead & Company.
Whistle For Willie, by Ezra Jack Keats. Copyright 1964 by Ezra Jack Keats. Reprinted by permission of Viking Penguin Inc.
The Mother from *Television Plays*. Copyright©1955 by Paddy Chayefsky; renewed©1983 by Susan Chayefsky; reprinted by permission of Simon and Schuster, Inc.
B. Johnson; "Durkheim's One Cause of Suicide"; ASR, vol. 30, 1965; p. 876. Reprinted by permission of The American Sociological Association.

CONTENTS

ACKNOWLEDGMENTS vii

LIST OF TABLES xiii

LIST OF PHOTOGRAPHS xv

LIST OF APPLIED THEATRE ACTIVITIES xvii

INTRODUCTION 1
   Demographic Overview 1
   The Problems of Aging 5
   Successful Adaptation to Aging: Theoretical Perspectives 10
   The "New Leisure Class": Creative Potential 11
   This Study 12

PART I:
THEORETICAL AND CONCEPTUAL OVERVIEW OF THE PROCESS AND PROBLEMS OF AGING

1 SOCIAL THEORIES OF AGING 21
   Disengagement Theory 21
   Activity Theory 25
   Social Integration Theory 27

2 CREATIVITY OVER THE LIFE SPAN 36
   Introduction and Review of the Literature 36
   Theoretical/Conceptual Models 47
   Examples of Creative Seniors 52

PART II:
APPLIED THEATRE ARTS AND THE ELDERLY

Introduction 65

3 COLLECTIVE IMAGES OF AGING:
   THE PLAYWRIGHT'S INFLUENCE 69
   The Greek Playwright's Image of Aging 70
   Shakespeare's Image of Aging 73
   The Restoration Playwright's Image of Aging 75
   The Modern Playwright's Images of Aging 77

4	**CREATIVE DRAMATICS**	83
	Pioneers of Creative Drama	85
	Children and Creative Drama	87
	Dramatic Play with Children	88
	Lifespan Aesthetic Assessment	89
	Creative Dramatics with Senior Adults	91
	Creative Dramatics-Implementation at Five Senior Adult Sites	92
5	**THEATRE TECHNIQUES WITH THE ELDERLY**	106
	Mirror Exercises	107
	Improvisational Theatre Technique	112
	Oral History Theatre	116
	Oral History Theatre Techniques	116
	Talking Book Series	123
	Intergenerational Participatory Theatre	128
	Original Scriptwriting	143
	Improvisational Scenework as a Mode for Playwriting	144
6	**APPLIED THEATRE TECHNIQUES WITH THE HANDICAPPED ELDERLY**	147
	Music Activities as an Applied Theatre Technique	148
	Dance-Movement Activities as an Applied Theatre Technique	153
	Visual Arts Activities as an Applied Theatre Technique	157
	Sociodrama as an Applied Theatre Technique	158

PART III:
AN ASSESSMENT OF THE IMPACT OF APPLIED THEATRE TECHNIQUES ON THE ELDERLY

7	**STUDY DESIGN AND METHODOLOGY**	163
	Subjects	163
	Dependent Variables	165
8	**DATA ANALYSIS AND FINDINGS**	169
	Quantitative Results	169

9 CONCLUSIONS AND SUGGESTIONS FOR FUTURE RESEARCH	175
Theoretical Implications and Directions for Future Research	176
The Role of the Artist in the Specific Experimental Design	178
Commitment to Interaction--Art/Science	179
Interaction and Shared Observation--Art/Science	179
Evaluation--Art/Science	180
APPENDIX	183
INDEX	193
ABOUT THE AUTHORS	203

LIST OF TABLES

Table 1
Changes in Numbers and Proportions of the U.S.
Population of those 65 and over from 1900-2030   2

Table 2
Percentage of Labor Force Participants by Age Group and
Sex, United States, 1900-1990   4

Table 3
Implementation of Applied Theatre Programs at
Site A: Establishing an Aesthetic Environment   102

Table 4
Implementation of Applied Theatre Programs at
Sites B and C: Establishing an Aesthetic Environment 103

Table 5
Implementation of Applied Theatre Programs at
Sites D and E: Establishing an Aesthetic Environment 104

Table 6
Demographic Characteristics of Study Participants   164

Table 7
Demographic Characteristics of Study
Participants at Each Site   165

Table 8
Mean Scores on Global Measure of Life Satisfaction   170

Table 9
Mean Scores on Loneliness   170

Table 10
Mean Scores on Subjective Age Identification   171

LIST OF PHOTOGRAPHS

Senior Actors	63
Whistle for Willie	127
Seniors Prepare Artwork	127
Canal Boats: Making Props	131
Canal Boats: The Ticket Taker	131
Fill-in-the-Blank Participatory Theatre: *One Hot Summer Day*. . . .	133
Fill-in-the-Blank Participatory Theatre: *In a Nearby Town Called*. . . .	135
Participatory Storybook Theatre	136
Children and Seniors	142
Lunch at the White House Cast Members	143
A Senior Actor-Playwright Takes a Break	144
Scarf-Chairdancing	155
The President Speaks	191

LIST OF APPLIED THEATRE ACTIVITIES

Mirror Exercise #1	107
Mirror Exercise--Specific Focus	107
Mirror Exercise--Undesignated Focus	108
Mirror Exercise--Group Focus	108
Mirror Exercise--Designated Emotion: Negative	109
Mirror Exercise--Designated Emotion: Positive	109
Mirror Exercise--Silent Partner	109
Group Poem--Free Verse	110
Group Poem--Seasonal	111
Group Poem--Feelings: Statues	111
Improvisation--Who, What, Where: "Stuck In"	113
Who, What, Where--Personal Experience	114
Who, What, Where--Character Focus	114
Oral History Theatre--Topics	116
Oral History Theatre--"Washington--This must Be Heaven"	119
Oral History Theatre--"Never Trust a Male Driver!"	119
Oral History Theatre--"My Fling With a Trapeze Artist"	119
Oral History Theatre--"Tales of Stormy Nights"	120
Oral History Theatre--"A Secret Kiss"	121
Talking Book Series--*Whistle for Willie*	124
Participatory Historical Theatre	128
Fill-in-the-Blank Participatory Theatre	132
Participatory Storybook Theatre	135
Original Scriptwriting	143
Musical Parts	149
Musical Characters	150
Musical Emotions	151
Found Sounds	151
Scarf-Chairdancing	153
Rhythm-Movement Master	154
Colordance	156
Choreopoem-Dance	156
Visual Arts	157
Sociodrama	158
Composition of the Day	185
Original Scripts	185
Splices of Life	185
Lunch at the White House	188

INTRODUCTION

DEMOGRAPHIC OVERVIEW

The United States has experienced nothing short of a demographic revolution during the nineteenth and twentieth centuries, resulting in what has been variously referred to as the maturing of our population by some and the "graying of the United States" by others. Since 1900 the number and percentage of the population sixty-five and over have increased dramatically, from approximately three million (representing four percent of the total population) in 1900, to 12 million in 1950, to 26 million today (representing 11 percent of the total population). The elderly segment of the population is growing faster than any other. The percentage of the population 65 and over has more than doubled since 1900 (from four percent to 11 percent) whereas the increase in actual numbers of those 65 and over has been eightfold (from three million to 26 million). In 1900, one out of every 25 Americans was 65 and over, compared to today when one of every nine is in that age group. In 2030 it is predicted that one in every five Americans will be 65 and over. Table 1 illustrates the dramatic increase since 1900 in the numbers of elderly and the proportion of the total population which they represent.

These demographic changes are the result of several technological, cultural, and scientific factors that accompanied the industrialization of society. High immigration rates prior to World War II were one factor that contributed to the increase. Scientific and medical breakthroughs, as well as improved sanitation and nutrition, have further prolonged life and reduced infant mortality, allowing many more today to live beyond age 65 than in any previous time in history. The dramatic increase in the number and percentage of elderly in our population is basically the result of changes in mortality and fertility rates. High birth rates of the nineteenth and twentieth centuries, coupled with decreased infant mortality rates and dramatically increased life expectancy, combine to explain the present demographic structure of the U.S. population.

Every day approximately 5000 Americans turn 65. Approximately 3600 Americans 65 and over die every day. The net increase is 1400 per day or 500,000 per year. This trend is expected to continue, resulting in an even larger number of individuals 65 and over, who will represent an even larger percentage of the total population in the future. By the year 2010 the elderly population in this country will soar as the post-World War II "baby boomers" enter the ranks of the elderly, creating a "senior boom" early in the twenty-first century. Sheppard and Rix (1977) in *The Graying of Working America* predict a 30 percent increase in the number of elderly between the years 2000 and 2030. They suggested that during that 30-year period the number of people 65 and over in the United States population may increase by over 100 percent.

TABLE 1. Changes in Numbers and Proportions of the U.S. Population of those 65 and over from 1900-2030

Year	Numbers 65+	Proportion of the U.S. Population
1900	3 million	4%
1980	26 million	11%
2000	32 million	13%
2030	52 million	20%

Source: U.S. Department of Health and Human Services, 1979.

INTRODUCTION / 3

People are living longer today than ever before in our nation's history. A child born in 1900 could expect to live approximately 45 years; a child born today can expect to live approximately 74 years (78 for females, 71 for males); almost a doubling of life expectancy. Life expectancy at age 65 has also increased--in fact it increased more between 1950 and 1980 than it had in the first half of the century. Life expectancy at age 65 in 1900 was 11.9 years; in 1980 it was 16 years. Thus, the average person today who has survived to 65 years can expect another 16 years of life (white males 13.7, white females 18.1, black males 13.8, black females 17.6). Demographers refer to this situation as mass longevity; never before in history has a society been faced with such numbers and percentages of older people.

Not only are more people living longer today than ever before, but they are also spending considerably more time outside of "productive" work in the labor force than previously in history. In 1900, two-thirds of the males 65 and over were still employed, compared to 44.6 percent in 1955, and 19 percent in 1981 (U.S. Bureau of the Census, 1980).

The male labor force participation rate decreased steadily from two in three older men in 1900 to one in five in 1978; the female rate rose slightly from one in 12 in 1900 to one in ten during the 1950s but dropped to one in 12 in the 1970s. Based on their comprehensive analysis of changing labor force participation in the United States from 1890 to 1970, Graney and Cottam (1981) conclude that labor force participation of males has declined by about five percent per decade between 1890 and 1970--a decline of more than forty percent during the eighty-year period. The decline in labor force participation by males, although initiated in the nineteenth century, accelerated after World War II, a period in which labor force participation of females increased greatly. Today, 80 percent of men and 90 percent of women 65 and over are outside the labor force--neither working nor looking for work.

Table 2 portrays the dramatically changing labor force participation rates for men and women over 45 since 1900.

These changes in labor force participation are due to historic changes in urbanization, compulsory education, technological advances, less self-employment (the move away from agriculture), mandatory retirement, and pension programs (Hendricks and Hendricks, 1977).

TABLE 2. Percentage of Labor Force Participants by Age Group and Sex, United States, 1900-1990

	Male		Female	
Date	45-64 years	65+ years	45-64 years	65+ years
1990*	84.5	19.3	51.9	8.3
1980*	85.5	21.2	50.4	8.6
1974	83.7	21.5	47.3	7.8
1970	87.2	25.8	48.2	9.2
1960	89.8	32.2	43.0	10.5
1940	89.4	42.2	20.0	6.0
1920	90.7	55.6	16.5	7.3
1900	90.3	63.1	13.6	8.3

*Projected

Sources: U.S. Bureau of Census, Statistical Abstract of the United States: 1975. 95th ed. (Washington, D.C.: U.S. Government Printing Office, 1975), p. 344; U.S. Bureau of Census, Historical Statistics of the United States, Colonial Times to 1957 (Washington, D.C.: U.S. Government Printing Office, 1960), p. 71. Taken from Hendricks and Hendricks, 1977, p. 68.

The institution of retirement is a relatively recent phenomenon, found only in modernized, industrialized countries. Even in the United States until fairly recently very few people lived long enough to retire, and most worked in agricultural or craft professions until they died or became too feeble to work. In many underdeveloped countries this is still the case. The word *retirement* was not even in use in 1900. Today, approximately 90 percent of all U.S. citizens intend to retire, and many are opting to retire early. In 1963, for example, 23 percent of those 45 to 54 years of age who were surveyed in a Harris poll said that they planned to retire early. In 1976, 41 percent between the age of 45 and 54 who were surveyed said they planned to retire early.

It is only in fairly recent times that large numbers of individuals have lived long enough to enter the retirement stage of the life cycle. In earlier times, when life expectancy was considerably shorter and Social Security was not available as economic support for individuals in retirement, there was substantially less time spent outside of involvement in the work force and in leisure. Until recently, for most people leisure has been more a problem of finding some than of worrying how to spend it, the situation facing large numbers of retirees today.

It is clear that, compared to other age groups, the elderly, who are no longer engaged in productive work in the labor force, have the largest amount of leisure time to be enjoyed--or endured. Most individuals living in the United States today can expect to spend about one-third of their lives in leisure, outside the work force. In his classic article entitled "The New Leisure Class," Michelon (1954) described our nation's elderly as the "new leisure class" and suggested that the major developmental task confronting the elderly is to find meaningful new roles and activities to replace those of work, raising a family, and overcoming day-to-day problems, which previously occupied them during their adult years.

In light of the fact that so many more people in the United States are reaching old age today and can expect to live longer than ever before, with considerably more leisure time, it is increasingly important to focus upon the problems, concerns, needs, and issues facing the elderly in our society. Increasing attention to productive, meaningful use of leisure time is another equally important concern that should be addressed.

In the next section of this chapter we examine some of the problems of growing old, particularly focusing on the situation of the elderly in U.S. society.

THE PROBLEMS OF AGING

Stephen Vincent Benét nicely captured the negative aspect of growing old in a short poem when he insightfully wrote:

A stone's a stone
And a tree's a tree
But what was the sense of aging me?
It's no improvement
That I can see.

Studies of older individuals have highlighted several categories of problems affecting the elderly including: physical, economic, and sociopsychological. Some of the major problems in the sociopsychological realm result primarily from the diminished social participation of the elderly in the sphere of work and family; rejection in the labor market; forced dependency on no-choice social services; and "sandbox" treatment in keep-them-busy programs. Old age is a period of multiple losses. Many older individuals lose vital social roles in the world of work, family, politics, and community. Accompanying the loss of the work role are the concomitant losses of income, power, status, and prestige. Many also experience physical losses in old age. Seventy-eight percent of the elderly have at least one chronic health condition. Declining health, loss of a limb or of one's eyesight can be almost impossible to bear. The pain of chronic debilitating illness racks the bodies of many in old age. Still others experience deep personal losses, such as the death of a spouse or close friend. The last stage of life often becomes a series of goodbyes as one sees older friends and relatives dying one by one.

In addition to the aforementioned maladies of old age--ill health, insufficient income, and social isolation--one also has to come to grips at this stage in the life cycle with one's own relatively imminent demise. The issues of death and dying assume a more prominent place in one's thoughts.

Loss of such an important role as the occupational role is potentially damaging to social interaction and personal identity because the loss of such a central role places the retired individual outside his or her normal group of patterned associations and takes away a major source of meaning. Some writers, most notably Stephen Miller (1965), have conceptualized the loss of the work role as a form of "identity crisis" for the male. Lopata (1973) and others have similarly considered widowhood an identity crisis for many older women, whose concept of self, schedule of activities, and friendship associations, all revolved around the husband.

Many older people thus find themselves living in a shrunken social world. Many of their friends and loved ones have died, and participation in organized clubs and social groups is usually considerably diminished from younger days. Elaborating upon the work of the classic sociologist Emile Durkheim, Irving Rosow (1967) suggests that, due to these losses of major roles and group involvements, the elderly experience a decrease in "social integration." They are, in other words, cut off from their society, not tied in, they are adrift and marginal. As a result, many experience feelings of loneliness, anxiety, uneasiness. Life loses all meaning for many of the elderly.

Old age, unlike other stages in the life cycle, is the first stage of life with systematic status loss. When one enters the later stages of life and assumes the aged role, loss of status is experienced as one realizes that the goals set in life may not have been achieved; and, as the means to achieve them dwindle, they may never be achieved.

Building on the early work of Durkheim, Rosow (1967) suggests that the elderly tend to be less integrated into society due to (1) their removal and withdrawal from certain organizational contexts and associated roles, which weakens their ties to mediating structures such as work, voluntary associations, and like organizations; and (2) the contraction of their intimate social world, which results from relocation, incapacitation, and death of friends and peers. In comparison to other age groups, the elderly belong to fewer formal and informal social groups, and also have fewer friendships (Rosow, 1967; Blau, 1973). Not only are the elderly less integrated into society, they are also more "anomic," to use Durkheim's term. The aged role is not clearly specified or structured, leaving the elderly in a position of not knowing which behaviors are expected and acceptable and which ones are not. For these reasons, Ernest Burgess has referred to the aged role in U.S. society as the "roleless role."

Related to the position of social integration theory derived from the symbolic interactionists' perspective, role theory (Lopata, 1973; Blau, 1973) posits that individuals derive an identity and sense of self through interaction with significant others in the performance of social roles in groups. Some sources of identity are more important than others; that is, some relationships, such as marriage, involve "significant others." According to Everett C. Hughes (1981, originally 1958), some roles are associated with "master status" and have a greater impact on the self and identity than others. The occupational role is a "master status" in our society, particularly for males.

Loss of social roles, according to this perspective, results in loss of identity and subsequent loss of esteem, lowered self-concept, and a sense of meaninglessness in life. Widowhood and retirement are viewed from this perspective as major losses of social roles that thrust the individual outside his or her normal group of patterned associations, which formerly served to locate incumbents in a matrix of other roles and provide a sense of identity and meaning.

In addition to declining health, shrinking finances, loss of social roles, friends, spouse, status, and power, the elderly in the United States also face all the problems of negative stereotyping and "ageism." As Robert Butler (1975) described the tragedy of growing old in the United States:

> For many elderly Americans old age is a tragedy, a period of quiet despair, deprivation, and desolation. . . . Herein lies what I consider to be the genuine tragedy of old age in America--We have shaped a society which is extremely harsh to live in when one is old (p. 2).

Cowgill and Holmes (1972) developed a cross-societal theory of aging demonstrating a strong relationship between level of modernization in society (based on level of technology, degree of urbanization, rate of social change, and degree of Westernization) and status of the aged. They demonstrated that in Western urban, industrial, technologically advanced societies the aged are devalued and hold less power, status, and economic control than in less advanced, more "backward" societies. Cowgill and Holmes's work and theory gained further support from Palmore and Manton's (1974) cross-cultural study in 31 countries, in which they convincingly demonstrated that the status of the aged is low in urban, industrialized countries, such as the United States (Quinney, 1965).

Rosow (1967) argues that the relative position of the aged in any society is governed by six institutional factors: (1) their ownership of property and control over the opportunities of the young; (2) their command of strategic knowledge and skills; (3) strong religiosity and sacred traditions; (4) strong kinship and extended family bonds in a communal or *Gemeinschaft* type of social organization; (5) a low productivity economy; and (6) high mutual dependence and reciprocal aid among members (p. 9). In U.S. society, according to Rosow, the aged suffer a loss of status on all these institutional dimensions.

U.S. society highly values youth and beauty, productivity, progress, speed, and independence. In his classic study of U.S. society, Robin Williams (1970) concluded that occupational success is not just one life goal among others in the United States but is *the* outstanding trait of the culture. Mizruchi's (1964) work further confirms the emphasis on work and success in our society. Retired from participation in the occupational role, the elderly suffer a severe loss of status, role, and power in our society, as well as loss of income.

The elderly in this country are often viewed as useless, dependent, nonproductive, a burden to be borne by younger members of the society. They are "over the hill, down the drain, out to pasture, fading fast" (Butler, 1975, p. 2). They are often the victims of ageism and negative stereotyping. Images of aging found in books, cartoons, well-known jokes and sayings, and the media present a picture of the elderly as sexless and senile, grumpy and toothless. As Lillian Troll suggests, the stereotype of elderly women in this country portray her as "poor," "dumb," and "ugly" (Troll, Israel, and Israel 1977). The elderly in this country are advised to buy creams to cover up "those ugly age spots and wrinkles," to join health and figure spas, and to try all sorts of diets to "keep that youthful figure". Hair dyes to "get rid of that ugly gray," dentures and tooth polish to "recapture that youthful smile," and tonics and pills to "feel young and look young again" are also available. If all these remedies fail to transform an old face and figure into a young one, the multibillion-dollar cosmetic business in the United States surely can perform the miracle.

In our youth-oriented, production-minded society the aged are devalued. Their skills become obsolete in the face of rapid technological change. Their wisdom and experience, gained from years of living, is of little or no use to the next generations, who confront a totally different world from the one in which their parents and grandparents lived.

How do the elderly view themselves in such a culture? Presumably, when all of the diets and pills and creams and cosmetics fail, the elderly are forced to see themselves as old. Indeed, many accept the negative cultural images and, consequently, their self-esteem and self-concept suffer.

It is not surprising that many older members of our society suffer from depression and loneliness, become unhappy, and, in extreme cases, even kill themselves. It is estimated that anywhere from 20 percent to 50 percent of the elderly in the United States are depressed. Depression increases steadily with age. Eighty percent of the elderly who commit suicide are depressed. The depression of the elderly is characterized by helplessness, hopelessness, and haplessness.

Several researchers have turned their attention to the loneliness of the elderly. The old adage "we are born alone and we die alone" is all too true for many elderly. Hyams (1969) noted that loneliness is very common in the elderly and can exert a profound influence in aggravating the emotional components of an illness by leading to feelings of insecurity and, later, apathy. Gaev (1976) identified the following factors as contributing to the loneliness of the aged: geographical isolation, language barriers, pain, loss, and fear of impending death. Weiss (1973) has identified an emotional and social component in loneliness. The loneliness of social isolation, according to Weiss, is the need for cohesive social networks. Retirement results in social loneliness and the retired individual feels shut out, shoved out, left out, and kept out. Ostrov and Offer (1980) write, "Loneliness can be described as a painful feeling of longing for another person or persons . . . as an inner craving for intimacy and closeness." Lopata (1980) has described the loneliness experienced by widows as an emotional and social experience in which there is a desperate need to be with the dead spouse, a longing for his presence, a need for companionship, but also a fracture in social networks and social role relationships, which places the widow outside her normal network of social interaction and isolates her socially. Lowenthal and Haven (1968) in their well-known study subtitled "Intimacy as a Critical Variable" discovered the importance of an "intimate" relationship or a confidant in warding off loneliness and depression and in increasing happiness and integration of the aged.

Statistics on suicide by age group in the United States reveal a dramatically high rate for our nation's elderly. Although they represent approximately 11 percent of the population, those 65 and over account for 25 percent of all suicides committed in this country (Resnick and Cantor, 1970). Mary Miller (1979) reports that about 10,000 people in the United States 60 and over kill themselves each year. Clearly, our elderly experience problems in their "golden" years.

SUCCESSFUL ADAPTATION TO AGING: THEORETICAL PERSPECTIVES

Gerontologists concerned with the myriad problems of growing old, discussed in the previous section, have offered several explanations of successful adaptation to aging. Three major theoretical perspectives exist in the literature. The first major theory, developed in the 1960s, suggests that disengagement from major social roles and positions, from involvement in groups and activities, and from involvement with family and friends is conducive to happiness in the later years. The disengagement theory has been severely criticized since it was initially proposed, and empirical research conducted during the past 20 years has, for the most part, failed to confirm the theory's validity. Two more recent social theories, developed primarily in response to the earlier theory of disengagement, suggest that elderly individuals who remain actively involved and engaged in social roles, groups, organizations, family, and community age more successfully than those who disengage or are disengaged by society. The activity theory, proposed in the 1970s, has largely been supported by empirical research conducted in the last ten years. Social integration theory, derived from the earlier work of Emile Durkheim and expanded in the writings of Irving Rosow (1967, 1973) and Nancy Osgood (1982), suggests that the most viable opportunities for social reintegration of the elderly in U.S. society are through association with age peers in age-based social groups and organizations or age-segregated housing projects and retirement communities. This social integration theory is similar to and builds upon activity theory in very important ways. The perspective suggests that it is through *activity* in age-segregated groups in the performance of meaningful social roles that the elderly become re-engaged and reintegrated into society and thus age more successfully. The theory suggests that age groups are peer groups and, thus, involvements in age-segregated groups or settings facilitate interaction and meaningful activity and involvement for the elderly. Chapter 1 presents an in-depth discussion of each of these major theories and relates each to the present study.

THE "NEW LEISURE CLASS": CREATIVE POTENTIAL

Simone de Beauvoir, in *The Coming of Age*, writes:

Old age exposes the failure of our entire civilization.
There is only one solution if old age is not to be an absurd
parody of our former life, and that is to go on pursuing
ends that give our existence meaning--devotion to individuals, to groups, or to causes, social, political, intellectual, or to creative work (p. 18).

Today's older U.S. citizens are a pioneer generation. They are the first group in our history to experience an abundant measure of free, unscheduled time. This new leisure is a product of technology, institutionalized retirement, and increased longevity. As Beauvoir so aptly points out, it is crucially important to harness the new leisure available to our elderly as a positive force and infuse the lives of these individuals with meaning. An important issue to be addressed is How can we as a society and as practitioners working with the elderly meet the new leisure needs so that available time becomes time to be enjoyed and fulfilled, rather than time to be endured or filled?

Gordon Strieb suggests that the expressive role (encompassing social, cultural, creative, religious, and recreational activities) is one of the most important roles in retirement for men and women (Strieb, 1956). Many 65 and over are no longer actively involved in the major instrumental roles in society, such as the work role. To be 65 today is quite a different experience from being 65 in the past in terms of health, education, and income. Whistler's mother was only 44 years old when her portrait was painted, and she was considered old. If we contrast her with Jane Fonda, who is also in her forties, we begin to get the idea that chronological age has undergone dramatic qualitative changes over the years. An adult of any age today in the United States is younger than a person of the same age in 1900. In 1900, many over forty would have considered themselves old, as many do in developing nations. Older people in the United States are physically healthier and better educated today than any previous generation. They are better able to appreciate the expressive roles and activities and to participate in creative recreational activities than former generations of elderly were.

Grandma Moses, Michaelangelo, Leonard Bernstein, George Bernard Shaw, Pablo Picasso, and countless others attest to the great creative potential of the later years. The task confronting gerontologists and practitioners today is to develop the creative potential of the elderly, our "new leisure class." Chapter 2 will present an in-depth discussion of creativity over the lifespan, reviewing the theoretical perspectives as well as the empirical literature available on the subject.

THIS STUDY

During the past ten years drama experts across the country have been using applied theatre as one way to provide meaningful experiences for senior adults. A quotation from *The Prophet* beautifully expresses the philosophy of applied theatre: "If he is indeed wise he does not bid you enter the house of his wisdom, but rather leads you to the threshold of your own mind" (Gibran, 1923).

Applied theatre is participatory drama that is spontaneous and expressive, created by the members of a group. The process of *doing* drama, and of *creating* images, scenes, and dialogue rather than a polished, memorized final play, characterizes creative dramatics. Creative dramatics was first introduced with children as a way to tap imagination and creativity and allow for self-exploration, emotional release, and fun. Creative dramatics is a continual discovery of ideas, thoughts, memories, talents, sayings, songs, colors, words, people, feelings, and sounds. It is for the moment, therefore it is ever-changing, developing, combining, meeting the needs of the group on a specific day, at a given time. As participatory drama it is created with and by the members of a group and therefore no final product is expected or required, other than whatever form is discovered or explored at the moment. Applied theatre with its lack of emphasis on a final product, and focus on the creative moment at hand, provides the participant with a fail safe experience. The fear of performing in front of a group of people is removed because in creative dramatics there is no audience. Performance, experience, and the ability to either recreate or interpret that experience, is talent. Thus, each participant has the talent of experience. Such an art form or leisure activity can be successfully participated in by the educated or uneducated, young and old.

In the last ten years creative dramatics has been used increasingly with seniors. The American Theatre Association first addressed the subject of adult theatre in 1973 when Vera Mowry Roberts, then association president, asked Paul Kozelka to chair the association's first committee on theatre for retirees. Since that time a lot has been happening in the aging-arts field. Senior theatre groups have sprung up all over the country. The Living Stage in Washington, D.C., involves seniors in improvisational theatre. Ruth Tate has been directing a group of seniors in White Plains, N.Y., which has won numerous awards in local theatre competitions. The Amber Area Arts Alliance of Amber, Pennsylvania, has been sponsoring a new project called Third Age Theatre that is a comprehensive dramatics program for individuals over 55. Another group called the College Avenue Players comprises adults ranging in age from 68 to 85 and has performed new plays to thousands of people throughout the East Bay area of San Francisco. In 1973, the National Council on the Aging (NCOA) created a special division, the Center on Arts and Aging. The division's purpose was to activate local and national groups to consider the important role that arts can play in life enrichment for the elderly. A large number of theatre groups, made up entirely of elderly players, was represented at the meetings of the National Council on the Aging-Arts that was held in January, 1978.

The increased involvement of the elderly in dramatics has recently become of interest to theatre leaders as well as gerontologists in national and regional organizations. This growing interest in applied theatre for the elderly, whether through creative dramatics, oral history theatre, or radio drama, has also brought about the need for research and the development of theatre techniques to be used with seniors. Paula Gross Gray (1974), as part of her doctoral dissertation, began to collect data concerning the effects of drama on the elderly. All groups of respondents--directors, staff, and participants in creative dramatics programs for the elderly--cited the following as major benefits to elderly participants: the opportunity to be of service to others; increased self-confidence that resulted from successful memorization and good performance; communication and social interaction skills developed through the group experience; and the emotional outlet provided by the experience. Martin Nolter (1973) offers support, based in his experience, for the use of creative dramatics techniques with the elderly. He writes: "Older persons should become involved in dramatics because it is an immediate creative experience which gives internal and external satisfaction."

The works of Isabelle Burger (1980), Patch Clark (1978), and others have demonstrated that seniors who participate in the creative drama experience have their lives changed. Many elderly who participate in the experience begin to communicate and see themselves as useful again. Life takes on new meaning for them.

As early as 1969, Dr. Stanley A. Czurles (1969), spokesman at a seminar on "Enlightening Retirement Living through the Arts," noted: "Age does not stop creative growth, its satisfactions, and developmental values. On the contrary, it frees the individual for the maximum personal involvement. The arts can help the elderly lead increasingly enriching lives."

Others working with seniors in applied theatre programs across the country have claimed benefits such as: improved memory, verbal, and cognitive skills; improved communication, socialization, and group skills; an improved sense of self and self-esteem; an emotional outlet; healthy, meaningful recreation and means of utilizing leisure time; and a way to achieve status, prestige, and self-fulfillment formerly acquired through performance of work and family roles.

The percentage of blacks among the aged is steadily growing. In 1960, blacks were 7.1 percent of all persons 65 and over; in 1980 they were 8.3 percent; and it is estimated that in the year 2000 they will be 9.5 percent of the elderly population (Williams, 1980). According to the U.S. Bureau of the Census, elderly blacks in the United States constitute the largest group of minority older people in the country, numbering 2,855,000 in 1979, which represents a 25 percent increase since 1970 (U.S. Bureau of the Census, 1980). There has been a dramatic increase in life expectancy at birth for blacks, from 33 years in 1900 to 60.8 years in 1950 to 69.2 years in 1978 (Soldo, 1980).

Due to their increased life expectancy, the increased percentage of the aged which they represent, and various social changes and policies of the recent past, black elderly are an ever growing "special population" whose leisure needs must be addressed. Recreational therapists and program directors working with aged blacks have in the past encountered numerous difficulties finding programs or therapies that work (*i.e.*, are accepted, participated in, and make a significant change in the lives of participants). Minority aged represent a unique and special population of elderly with particular skills and life experiences, problems and concerns, handicaps and deficits. Unfortunately, many recreational programs planned for minority elderly have a built-in white, middle-class bias and require certain skills or aptitudes (such as ability to read or write or appreciation for particular events or arts) or interests or tastes that many minority elderly do not possess.

Applied theatre represents a particularly appropriate activity for minority elderly because it utilizes the knowledge, skills, and talents of each person in the drama group and provides a fail safe experience that does not necessarily require reading ability, particular cultural aptitudes or tastes, or other skills. According to Dancy (1977), who identifies major strengths of the black elderly, two strengths of elderly blacks, which make them good candidates to benefit from participation in creative dramatics, are (1) the accumulation of wisdom, knowledge, and common sense about life that comes not only from age, but from the experience of hardship and suffering and (2) a creative genius in doing much with little.

Although the works of Gray, Nolter, and others offer testimonies to support drama programs by, with, and for the elderly, no systematic evaluation of the use of applied theatre with the elderly has been conducted. Controlled research investigating the effects of creative dramatics on the elderly is badly needed. As *Older Americans on Stage* (1979), the report to the Alliance for Arts Education of the American Theatre Association Senior Adult Theatre Project, states: "At least three kinds of formal research are needed: the first is controlled empirical studies measuring the impact of specific theatre strategies--improvisation, specific memorization techniques." Cornish (1978) similarly argued for controlled, systematic research on the effects of creative dramatics on the elderly in his article entitled "Senior Adult Theatre The State of the Art and a Call for Research."

This book reports the results of the first controlled, scientific investigation of the impact of applied theatre on the elderly. The major objective of the study reported upon in this work was to assess the effect of participation in weekly applied theatre sessions on the life satisfaction, self-perceived loneliness, and subjective age identification of elderly participants.

In order to test the effects of participation on seniors, a sample of 103 elderly individuals, 95 percent of whom were black, was chosen to participate in a weekly applied theatre program for approximately ten months. A matched control group (matched to study participants) of 27 elderly people was also chosen. The elderly in the control group were matched on the following major variables: age, race, health, marital status, education, and occupation.

Participants were chosen by contacting the directors of nutrition sites in Richmond and northern Virginia. Seven nutrition centers were chosen for the final study, two in Richmond and five in Alexandria and Arlington. At the five sites in northern Virginia the drama sessions were conducted by a qualified and experienced expert in theatre arts and senior theatre. Trained volunteers who were members of the staff conducted the sessions at the two Richmond sites. As a result, more detailed site descriptions and broader application of dramatics techniques are available for the five sites in northern Virginia than for the Richmond sites. The matched controls were chosen from another Richmond center.

Applied theatre techniques employed in the sessions included: *oral history theatre*, which is a collection of personal stories transposed into scripts for the stage and for sharing and discussion; *group poetry*, which is original poetry created and written together by a group; *improvisation*, which is the creation of scripts and dialogues using spontaneous expression and movement; *intergenerational theatre*, which involves children and seniors together in the dramatization of themes, stories, and books; *talking book series*, which involves oral/visual projects whereby children's books are transposed into radio scripts accompanied by acetate drawings and shown with the use of an overhead projector; *creative writing*, which involves imaginative sentence completions, creation of stories, dialogue, and scripts; *movement*, which involves interpretive dance, exercises, and other physical involvements using the senses and various parts of the body; and *visual art*, which involves the creation of book covers, acetate drawings, and props and scenery used in intergenerational theatre scenes. Some of the groups also performed before audiences.

Participants and nonparticipants were pretested and posttested using a global question on life satisfaction, as well as questions assessing self-perceptions of loneliness and subjective age identification.

Pretest and posttest data were computer analyzed using analysis of change scores to determine whether or not members of the experimental group changed significantly more than members of the control group after participation in the ten-month program. To calculate change scores we subtracted the mean score at Time 1 from the mean score at Time 2 for experimental and control groups and calculated the change in means for each group. A one-tailed t test of differences in changed means was then applied to test for statistical significance of change from Time 1 to Time 2 (Campbell and Stanley, 1963).

Two types of data were collected in the study, qualitative and quantitative. The drama leader at each site kept a detailed diary, recording observed changes in individual members of the group as well as group processes and problems. Participants were also interviewed and asked how they felt about the drama experience, how their lives had changed or if they had. Systematic observations were recorded by the group leader on a regular basis and kept in a journal.

Analysis of quantitative and qualitative data revealed significant positive changes in elderly participants in the applied theatre groups compared to those in the control group. Parts II and III of this book are devoted to in-depth discussions of the design, implementation, and evaluation of the applied theatre program, as well as of major findings from analysis of qualitative and quantitative data collected.

This book is intended for several audiences. The practitioner in therapeutic recreation or arts therapy, as well as program directors at nursing homes, day care centers, community centers, churches, retirement communities and homes, and at other settings working with the elderly will find the book useful as a manual for design and implementation of a weekly program of applied theatre with senior adults. They will also find sample exercises, drama activities and techniques, and sample "products" created by participants in the weekly groups. Those working with the elderly using creative therapies in general and creative drama, in particular, will, for the first time, have scientific documentation that such techniques and programs actually make a difference in the lives of elderly participants. Statistically significant changes on important dependent variables are documented.

The book makes an empirical and theoretical contribution to the field of aging. The results of this empirical study are related to the larger body of knowledge and theory concerning recreation and leisure, creativity across the lifespan, loneliness, morale, and subjective age identification of the elderly, and social integration and activity theory.

The major contribution of this book is as a bridge between the arts and sciences. The design, implementation, evaluation, and reporting of this study was conducted jointly by an artist and a scientist, each contributing unique and different perspectives, sets of skills and talents, backgrounds, and knowledge. The interrelationship of arts and science, the artist and the scientist, is evident throughout the book.

REFERENCES

Beauvoir, S. 1972. *The Coming of Age.* Translated by Patrick O'Brian. New York: Putnam.

Blau, Z. 1973. *Old Age in a Changing Society.* New York: New Viewpoints.

Burger, I. 1980. *Creative Drama for Senior Adults.* Wilton, Connecticut: Morehouse-Barlow.

Butler, R. 1975. *Why Survive? Being Old in America.* New York: Harper & Row.

Campbell, B. T., and Stanley, J. C. 1963. "Experimental and quasiexperimental designs for research." In *Handbook of Research and Teaching*, edited by N. L. Gage. Chicago, Rand McNally.

Clark, P. 1978. "Theatre Arts and the Aging." Master's Thesis presented to the Theatre Department of Virginia Commonwealth University, Richmond, Virginia.

Cornish, R. M. 1978. "Senior Adult Theatre--The State of the Art and a Call for Research." *Theatre News* (May):1-11.

Cowgill, D., and L. Holmes (Editors). 1972. *Aging and Modernization.* New York: Appleton-Century-Crofts.

Czurles, S. 1969. "Enriching Retirement Living through the Arts." Paper presented at Union College, Schenectady, New York, June 19-21, 1969.

Dancy, J., Jr. 1977. *The Black Elderly: A Guide for Practitioners.* Ann Arbor, Michigan: University of Michigan Press.

Durkheim, E. 1964. *The Division of Labor in Society.* Translated by George Simpson. New York: Free Press.

———. 1951. *Suicide.* Translated by John A. Spaulding. New York: Free Press.

Gaev, D. 1976. *The Psychology of Loneliness.* Chicago: Adams.

Gibran, K. 1923. *The Prophet.* New York: Alfred A. Knopf.

Graney, M., and D. Cottam. 1981. "Labor Force Nonparticipation of Older People: United States 1890-1970." *The Gerontologist* 21:138-141.

Gray, P. 1974. *Dramatics for the Elderly: A Guide for Residential Care Settings and Senior Centers.* New York: Teachers College, Columbia University.

Harris, L., and Associates. 1975. *The Myth and Reality of Aging in America.* Washington, D.C.: The National Council on the Aging, Inc.

Hendricks, J., and C. Hendricks. 1977. *Aging in Mass Society: Myths and Realities.* Cambridge, Massachusetts: Winthrop.

Hughes, E. C. 1981. *Men and Their Work.* Westport, Connecticut: Greenwood Press (reprint of 1958 edition).

Hyams, D. E. 1969. "Psychological Factors in Rehabilitation of the Elderly." *Gerontologica Clinica* 11:129-136.

Lopata, H. 1973. *Widowhood in an American City.* Cambridge, Massachusetts: Schenkman Publishing Co.

———. 1980. "Loneliness in Widowhood." In *The Anatomy of Loneliness,* edited by J. Hartog, J. Audy, and Y. Cohen, pp. 237-259. New York: International University Press.

Lowenthal, M., and C. Haven. 1968. "Interaction and Adaptation: Intimacy as a Critical Variable." *American Sociological Review* 33:20-30.

Michelon, L. 1954. "The New Leisure Class." *American Journal of Sociology* 59:371-378.

Miller, M. 1979. *Suicide After Sixty: The Final Alternative.* New York: Springer Verlag.

Miller, S. 1965. "The Social Dilemma of the Aging Leisure Participant." In *Older People and Their Social World,* edited by A. Rose and W. Peterson, pp. 77-92. Philadelphia: F. A. Davis.

Mizruchi, E. 1964. *Success and Opportunity.* New York: Free Press.

Nolter, M. 1973. "Drama for the Elderly: They Can Do It." *The Gerontologist* 12:153-156.

Older Americans on Stage. 1979. Report to the Alliance for Arts Education of the American Theatre Association Senior Adult Project. Washington, D.C.

Osgood, N. 1982. *Senior Settlers: Social Integration in Retirement Communities*. New York: Praeger.
Ostrov, E., and D. Offer. 1980. "Loneliness and the Adolescent." In *The Anatomy of Loneliness*, edited by J. Hartog, J. Audy, and Y. Cohen, pp. 170-186. New York: International University Press.
Palmore, E., and K. Manton. 1974. "Modernization and Status of the Aged: International Correlations." *Journal of Gerontology* 29:205-210.
Quinney, R. 1965. "Suicide, Homicide and Economic Development." *Social Forces* 43:401-408.
Resnick, H., and J. Cantor. 1970. "Suicide and Aging." *Journal of the American Geriatrics Society* 18:152-158.
Rosow, I. 1973. "The Social Context of the Aging Self." *The Gerontologist* 12:82-87.
_____. 1967. *Social Integration of the Aged*. New York: Free Press.
Sheppard, H., and S. Rix. 1977. *The Graying of Working America: The Coming Crisis of Retirement and Policy*. New York: Free Press.
Soldo, B. 1980. "America's Elderly in the 1980's." *Population Bulletin* Number 35. Washington, D.C.: Population Reference Bureau, Inc.
Strieb, G. 1956. "Morale of the Retired." *Social Problems* 3:270-276.
Troll, L., J. Israel, and K. Israel. 1977. *Looking Ahead: A Woman's Guide to the Problems and Joys of Growing Older*. Englewood Cliffs, New Jersey: Prentice-Hall.
United States Bureau of the Census. 1980. *Statistical Abstract of the United States*. Washington, D.C.: U.S. Government Printing Office.
United States Department of Health and Human Services, Office of Human Development, Administration on Aging. 1979. *Facts About Older Americans, 1979*. Washington, D.C.: USGPO Publication Number 80-20006.
Weiss, R. 1973. *Loneliness: The Experience of Emotional and Social Isolation*. Cambridge, Massachusetts: MIT Press.
Williams, B. 1980. *Characteristics of the Black Elderly--1980. Statistical Reports on Older Americans*. Washington, D.C.: U.S. Government Printing Office.
Williams, R., Jr. 1970. *American Society*. New York: Alfred A. Knopf.

I

THEORETICAL AND CONCEPTUAL OVERVIEW OF THE PROCESS AND PROBLEMS OF AGING

1

SOCIAL THEORIES OF AGING

A main question addressed by social gerontologists is: What factors promote or inhibit successful aging? In the sociopsychological literature of gerontology there are several points of view or theories regarding optimum patterns of aging. As Maddox (1963) pointed out: "The relationship between activity and morale has been a perennial subject of research in the field of gerontology" (p. 195). Most often there has been a concern with the effect of loss of social roles and decreases in activity on life satisfaction (or morale, happiness, or successful aging). In this chapter we will discuss three major social theories of aging: disengagement theory, activity theory, and social integration theory. This study, discussed in following chapters, provides a partial test of each of these theoretical perspectives.

DISENGAGEMENT THEORY

The first formally stated social theory of aging is the disengagement theory found primarily in its original formulation by Cumming and Henry (1961) in *Growing Old: The Process of Disengagement.* Based on a five-year study of 275 people between the ages of 50 and 90, who were in good health and had the minimum money needed for independence, disengagement theory referred to aging as:

> ... an inevitable mutual withdrawal or disengagement, resulting in decreased interaction between the aging person

and others in the social system he belongs to. The process may be initiated by the individual or by others in the situation. The aging person may withdraw more markedly from some classes of people while remaining relatively close to others. His withdrawal may be accompanied from the outset by a preoccupation with himself; certain institutions in society may make this withdrawal easy for him. When the aging process is complete, the equilibrium which existed in middle life between the individual and his society has given way to a new equilibrium characterized by a greater distance and an altered type of relationship (p. 14).

Cumming and Henry discovered that older individuals gradually withdraw from social interaction and involvement in groups, organizations, and roles characteristic of middle age, and they turn their attention inward, focusing concern on the self. Disengagement was seen as an intrinsic developmental process that was biologically based, a response to declining energy and shrinking life space, both of which characterize the aging process. The theory contends that it is normal and positive for people to decrease their activity and seek more passive roles as they age. It also suggests that the individual and society mutually agree to prepare for the time when serious illness or death will cause a final disengagement. A gradual withdrawal by both the individual and society makes it possible to maintain the two in equilibrium. Thus, when death comes the individual feels freed of societal functions and obligations; and society does not experience a severe disruption. It is also suggested that both society and the older individual derive a sense of satisfaction from this decreased involvement. This process, which is inevitable and universal, is readily accepted by the individual and facilitates successful aging.

Theorists of disengagement were greatly influenced by the school of theory known as functionalism (or structural functionalism). Functionalism, one of the oldest sociological theories, has been used in biology, psychology, and anthropology. Employing an organic analogy, structural functionalists view society as a smoothly functioning system. Every process, institution, and configuration of roles and relationships contributes to the overall functioning of the social system, just as digestion, respiration, and other physiological processes are necessary for an organism to function.

The best statement of the meaning of the term *function* can be found in Emile Durkheim's *The Rules of Sociological Method* (1950):

> When . . . the explanation of a social phenomenon is undertaken, we must seek separately the efficient cause which produces it and the function it fulfills. We use the word "function," in preference to "end" or "purpose," precisely because social phenomena do not generally exist for the useful results they produce. We must determine whether there is a correspondence between the fact under consideration and the general needs of the social organism, and in what this correspondence consists, without occupying ourselves with whether it has been intentional or not (p. 95).

The concept of function thus implies "needs" of the social system, which are fulfilled by some particular social process. Employing this type of analysis, Durkheim discussed the functions of the division of labor in society as integrative or contributing to social solidarity, and he described the four functions of religion in society as: disciplinary, cohesive, revitalizing, and euphoric (Durkheim, 1954).

Talcott Parsons, the leading exponent of functionalism in U.S. sociology, first applied the theory to the process of aging in a 1960 paper and later in a brief essay written in 1963. According to Parsons, U.S. society has certain functional requirements, one of which is to have people in key positions who will be able to carry out their jobs without interruption. Therefore, disengagement of the old (who are closer to death) is a functional necessity if the society is to continue in equilibrium and satisfies the needs of the social system. Parsons also points out that our system of values emphasizes youth, newness, productivity, and materialism. Instrumental activities, such as we in the United States value, emphasize physical strength and agility and thus favor the young over the old. Parsons views disengagement as a case of freeing the old from ascriptive ties, which is a central theme in the development of advanced societies (Parsons, 1960, p. 172). Old age is described as a "consummatory" phase of life in which older individuals are free to enjoy the harvests of life without the burden of social participation and power (Parsons, 1963).

Disengagement is a functionalist theory. Disengagement is viewed as functional for society and for older individuals. The process is functional for society because (1) it eliminates the turmoil, disruption, and disequilibrium caused by the death of a fully engaged person and assures an uninterrupted continuation of the social system and an orderly transition of power from older to younger members; and (2) it opens up slots in the social and economic system for young individuals, who have more up-to-date knowledge and skills and are more dependable because they are less likely to die. The process is functional for the older individual because (1) he or she has less energy to perform major social roles and carry out activities in groups and organizations; and (2) he or she realizes that skills and capacities to function effectively are declining and death is imminent. Those individuals who achieve a new sense of equilibrium characterized by greater psychological distance, altered types of relationships, and decreased social interaction are the happiest in late life.

Disengagement theory generated much criticism and controversy from the time it was first proposed. Hochschild (1975) criticized the theory on logical grounds claiming that the theory provides an "escape clause." Any evidence of engaged oldsters can be refuted as examples of exceptions or of those off in their timing. Maddox (1963) pointed out that Cumming and Henry's study was cross-sectional rather than longitudinal and utilized a sample that was not representative. Thus their findings may be an artifact of systematic bias in the distribution of antecedent and intervening factors.

The theory has also been criticized for its claims that disengagement is universal and inevitable. Rose (1964) suggested that the theory is ethnocentric and reflects the bias of an industrial society. Other opponents point to the Abkhasians and Japanese as societies that offer greater opportunities for engagement of older members and, as a result, older members remain actively involved in roles and relationships in such societies. Politics in U.S. society is cited as another example that refutes the claims that disengagement is universal and inevitable. Many politicians who remain actively engaged are in the later stages of the life cycle. Similarly, emeritus professors remain actively engaged (Roman and Taietz, 1967).

Others argue that such a theory ignores personality and temperamental differences among older individuals (Maddox, 1964). Butler (1976) has called the theory a myth. It is important to remember that the disengagement theory was developed based on research with individuals who were old in the 1950s. These older individuals faced a different set of social conditions and past influences than do older individuals today. Social security benefits are better today and many more people have been retired and can serve as role models. Older individuals today have been better educated and have experienced better health. For these reasons, the theory may have been a better explanation for aging earlier but certainly does not apply as well to the elderly of the 1980s.

Perhaps the most important critique of disengagement theory is that most empirical research has failed to support its major tenets. Several studies, which have examined the relationships between social activity or participation, self-concept, and morale, have demonstrated that disengagement is more often a function of lack of opportunity to be involved than of aging *per se* (Carp, 1968; Roman and Taietz, 1967; Kerns, 1980; Atchley, 1971; Desroches and Kaiman, 1964) and that those who remain actively engaged in social roles, groups, and activities are significantly happier and have more positive self-concepts than those who disengage (Carp, 1978; Havighurst, Neugarten, and Tobin, 1968; Graney, 1975; Palmore, 1968; Havighurst, 1961; Maddox, 1963; Gregory, 1983; Knapp, 1977; Maguire, 1983; Elliott, 1984).

The controversy over and lack of empirical support for disengagement theory resulted in the formal statement of the activity theory of aging about ten years after the appearance of disengagement theory.

ACTIVITY THEORY

Although the formal statement of activity theory did not appear in the literature until after disengagement theory, previous studies conducted in the 1950s and 1960s (Havighurst and Albrecht, 1953; Kutner *et al.*, 1956; Havighurst, 1961) had already revealed a strong positive correlation between remaining active and being happy. The basic premise of the activity theory of aging is that the older person who stays active in groups and organizations ages optimally and remains happy. The theory espouses the U.S. formula for happiness: "Keep active to remain happy!"

Activity theory, which has been called the "dominant paradigm in the field" (Decker, 1980), suggests that older individuals are essentially the same as middle-aged and younger individuals and have the same psychological and social needs: all individuals need to stay active and involved with people in social groups and organizations, to resist shrinkage of their life space and social involvement, and to find substitutes for lost roles in work, family, and community in order to maintain a sense of personal identity and positive self-concept and to maintain social support and affirmation of themselves as valuable, useful human beings. As Havighurst, Neugarten, and Tobin (1968) stated the position:

> . . . older people are the same as middle-aged people with essentially the same psychological and social needs. In this view, the decreased social interaction that characterizes old age results from the withdrawal by society from the aging person, and the decrease in interaction proceeds against the desires of most aging men and women. The older person who ages optimally is the person who stays active and manages to resist the shrinkage of his social world. He maintains the activities of middle age as long as possible and then finds substitutes for those activities he is forced to relinquish (p. 161).

The activity theory has its basis within the symbolic interactionist school of sociological theory, which emphasizes the importance of social role involvement and communication with others in social groups to self-concept and personal well-being. George Herbert Mead (1934), Charles Horton Cooley (1964), and other symbolic interactionists all maintain that the self emerges, develops, and is maintained through social interaction with others. It is through communication and social discourse with others in social groups that each of us comes to know what are appropriate and inappropriate behaviors and to confirm and reaffirm our identity and image of our self. Social activity is the very core of our lives according to symbolic interactionists.

Symbolic interactionists claim that a person's well-being is derived from participation in social groups because people are tied to groups by occupying positions in these groups and adhering to the roles that they are expected to play in group contexts. Playing roles provides for the development of personal identities through the process of role taking, that is, of sharing the viewpoint of another. By interacting with others playing contemporary roles one acts out and sustains an identity. When the other ceases to exist, one's identity also ceases to exist because its locus, as it were, was formed in the process of interaction between the self and the other.

Theories of symbolic interaction provide certain basic assumptions about the construction of social reality, including self-identity as it emerges in social interaction (Berger and Luckman, 1966; Blumer, 1969; McCall and Simmons, 1966). These assumptions are: (1) that identities are formulated in a complicated process of social interaction that involves symbolic definitions of the self, the other, and the situation; (2) that repeated interaction with the same other in similar situations results in a definite and stable self and other identities; (3) these identities are modified as the self, the other, or the definition of the situation change; and (4) the removal of the "significant others" from interaction with the self will necessitate a reformulation of the identities in which he or she was involved.

Borrowing from the concepts and ideas of this school of thought, Lemon, Bengtson, and Peterson (1972) put forth an axiomatic statement of the activity theory:

> Activity provides various role supports necessary for reaffirming one's self concept. The more intimate and the more frequent the activity, the more reinforcing and the more specific will be the role supports. Role supports are necessary for the maintenance of a positive self-concept, which in turn is associated with high life satisfaction (p. 519).

According to the activity theory, which has largely been supported by empirical research, participation in a weekly creative drama group would be beneficial for the elderly. Such participation would provide social discourse, reaffirmation of personal identity, role support, enhanced self-concept, and higher life satisfaction. Participation in such a group could provide a substitute for roles formerly played in family, work, and community and could help offset the disturbance in interaction patterns, social rewards, and negative self-image occasioned by the loss of these important social roles.

SOCIAL INTEGRATION THEORY

The third major social theory of aging to be discussed in this chapter is the social integration theory proposed by Irving Rosow (1967) and expanded upon by Nancy Osgood (1982). The social integration theory of aging, which posits a strong positive relationship between associating with or living among age peers and morale in late life, is derived in part from the earlier theory of social integration found in the writings of the classic French sociologist, Emile Durkheim.

Durkheim's interest in social integration stems from the theoretical premise that social integration is necessary both for the maintenance of the social order and the happiness of individuals

(Durkheim, 1951). In *Suicide*, Durkheim suggested that happiness depends upon one's finding a sense of meaning outside oneself that occurs only in the context of group involvement. Durkheim sought explanations for variations in the suicide rate in terms of the degree to which humans are integrated into society and the extent to which their conduct is regulated (Giddens, 1971). He maintained that high suicide rates appear with certain broad societal conditions such as malintegration and lack of social regulation. He derived two major propositions, namely (1) that the suicide rate varies inversely with the degree of integration of the group; and (2) that the suicide rate varies with the degree of normative regulation. After an examination of suicide statistics for different groups, Durkheim was able to demonstrate that Protestant countries had the highest suicide rate and Catholic countries the lowest and that countries with the highest divorce rates had the highest suicide rate. He concluded that integration into family, religious, and political groups is an important deterrent to suicide.

A close examination of the concept of integration reveals that what Durkheim called integration has something to do with a person's social ties to the larger group, with that person's level of meaningful interaction with other members of the larger social group, with that person's degree of social "belongingness." As he stated it:

> A society, group, or social condition is said to be integrated to the degree that its members possess a "common conscience" of shared beliefs and sentiments, interact with one another, and have a sense of devotion to common goals. In a condition of weak integration, life derives no meaning and purpose from the group (quoted in Johnson, 1965, p. 876).

The concept of integration refers to personal involvement in social groups, activities, and organizations. Persons who are deeply and intimately involved with others in various personal relationships and group activities, according to Durkheim, should be low suicide risks. Maris (1969) similarly defines integration in terms of the number of interpersonal dependency relationships in which the person is involved. Durkheim found the unmarried to have the highest rates of suicide, supporting his contention that those who are not integrated into society are at risk for suicide.

Several gerontologists, most of them sociologists, have translated some of the major concepts of the theoretical framework presented in the major works of the classic sociologists into various theories of aging. They have applied these to the particular case of retirement housing in an attempt to understand and explain life in these communities. Most gerontologists devising theories have sought to explain the higher level of morale that is consistently demonstrated empirically when life satisfaction of retirement community residents is measured or compared with morale of their counterparts in age-integrated settings.

The most elaborate statement of the integration theory of aging is stated in the work of Irving Rosow (1967). Rosow's basic contention is that elderly individuals' integration into the society as a whole is seriously weakened in several respects: loss of work role and subsequent loss of economic resources, loss of spouse and friends who die, and informal age grading that places a great distance between generations. The solution for reintegration of the nation's elderly, in Rosow's opinion, lies in age-segregated communities in which elderly individuals find a ready source of friends in age peers, as well as meaningful leisure roles and roles in various organizations. Rosow popularized the notion of "concomitant socialization" when he indicated that the most viable opportunities for the integration of older people are through informal groups among their age peers (Rosow, 1967, pp. 35-36).

According to Rosow, the integration of individuals into their society results from forces that place them within the system and govern their participation and patterned associations with others. This network of social bonds has three basic dimensions: social values, group memberships, and social roles. In other words, "people are tied into their society essentially through their beliefs, the groups that they belong to and the positions they occupy or their social roles" (Rosow, 1967, p. 162). Rosow's basic contention is that constant association with age peers or living among age peers provides the basis of social integration for older individuals. As he writes:

> The integration theory of aging follows the general premises and major findings of our study. People's self images and identifications reflect their actual group memberships. Accordingly, to the extent that integration into groups is related to residential concentration, identification will similarly be correlated with density. Presumably, under high density conditions, older neighbors are salient and people are aware of them. This increases their interaction and strong group ties. Density fosters the by-products of group life: consciousness of similarity; embeddedness in a bounded system; development of special group norms; role

specification and restructuring; generation of group supports, including workaday and emergency mutual aid and reciprocity; provision of significant reference figures and viable role models; stimulation of affiliative sentiments, and so on (Rosow, 1967, p. 261).

Rosow developed the social integration theory based on his empirical research. In his pioneering study of the effects of age-segregation on morale, Rosow investigated the life satisfaction of elderly residents in apartment buildings in Cleveland, Ohio. He classified living environments according to the density of elderly population as Normal, Concentrated, and Dense. He found that those living in the apartments that were more densely populated with elderly residents made more friends, which he attributed to the fact that friends are made among one's age and sex peers. They also experienced a higher level of life satisfaction and housing satisfaction. He further cited the following major social gains for those living among age peers: opportunities for remarriage, new identifications and mutual support, the facilitation of transition to a new role, the generation of new activities, and more appropriate behavioral norms.

Other investigators who have turned their attention to the issue of life satisfaction and age-segregated living have found support for Rosow's social integration theory. Aldridge (1959), Michelon (1954), Seguin (1973), Sheley (1974), Bultena and Wood (1969), Sherman (1975), and Sherman, et al. (1968) found high levels of morale among residents of age-segregated communities that they have studied. Comparative studies of residents and nonresidents have discovered that those living in age-segregated communities have higher levels of morale that their counterparts living in age-integrated communities.

Qualitative studies of life in age-segregated communities for the elderly have provided further support for Rosow's theory. Arlie Russell Hochschild (1973), who studied one small community, discovered sibling bonds among elderly residents and a working mutual aid society in which exchanges of services were reciprocal--"the many small, quiet favors, keeping an eye out for a friend and sharing a good laugh" (p. 409). Further support has recently been provided by Osgood's (1982) comparative study of life in three planned retirement communities (a mobile home community in Florida, a condominium complex in Florida, and a community of detached dwelling units in Arizona). Osgood found that in each community a strong "sense of community" developed. Everyone felt their lives were interconnected, with a common purpose and group loyalty to the community and to each other. Residents shared a common past, present, and future. They had similar values, interests, needs, concerns, and problems. They had raised their children, gone through the years of the Great Depression, and shared other social, cultural, and historical events. At this time in their lives they faced similar problems of rising costs and limited incomes, health and medical problems, retirement, widowhood, and the approach of death. Based on the in-depth study of life in the three communities, which differed on several important dimensions such as location, type of dwelling unit, background and characteristics of residents, and activities available, Osgood concluded that age *per se* served as the primary basis for the high levels of social integration found in each community.

In a similar vein, Eisenstadt (1956), Merton (1957), and Messer (1967) have argued that age-concentrated environments have the potential to become normative systems for residents, alleviating role conflict by insulating the activities of residents from those members of their "role-set" who occupy different status positions. Messer claims that a physical environment that segregates older individuals serves as a buffer to the conflicting role expectations of a younger population. In such an environment leisure pursuits become legitimate, as opposed to the work ethic accepted in the larger society. Such an orientation is much more conducive to those who find themselves retired. Bultena and Wood (1969) indeed discovered that normative attitudes of residents of such communities differed considerably from attitudes held by elderly individuals living in age-integrated communities, which he offers as support for the view that age-concentrated environments offer a source of normative attitudes to members. He attributed this fact to the abundance of role models exemplifying a positive orientation to leisure roles and the relative insulation from the work ethic.

Rose and Peterson (1965) and others have noted the development of an aged subculture, facilitated by age-segregated living. Rose and Peterson suggest that this subculture "provides a network of interrelationships and serves as a social and cultural milieu for the older individual" (p. 64). As they put it: "Not only can the potential range of social relationships be expanded, but also age-segregated living can provide socialization into and favorable evaluation of age-linked roles. . ." (p. 252). They also noted the importance of shared values in facilitating the aging process.

Living among age peers certainly provides the best conditions for social integration and the development of an aged subculture; however, some of the same benefits can be realized through regular association with age peers in various social groups and activities. Meeting with age peers on a regular basis, particularly in situations in which opportunities for mutual sharing, intimacy, and interaction exist and when issues of mutual concern such as age and aging and death and dying are a focus of discussion can facilitate social integration of elderly individuals. Weekly participation with age peers in creative dramatics groups might provide a viable opportunity for fostering social integration among elderly participants. We will examine this possibility in this study.

REFERENCES

Aldridge, G. 1959. "Informal Social Relationships in a Retirement Community." *Marriage and Family Living* 21:70-72.

Atchley, R. C. 1971. "Disengagement Among Professors." *Journal of Gerontology* 26:476-480.

Berger, P., and T. Luckman. 1966. *The Social Construction of Reality*. Garden City, New York: Anchor Books.

Blumer, H. 1969. *Symbolic Interactionism: Perspective and Method*. Englewood Cliffs, New Jersey: Prentice-Hall.

Bultena, G., and V. Wood. 1969. "The American Retirement Community: Bane or Blessing?" *Journal of Gerontology* 24:209-217.

Butler, R. 1976. *Why Survive?* New York: Harper & Row.

Carp, F. 1978. "Effects of Living Environment on Activity and Use of Time." *Aging and Human Development* 9:75-91.

_____. 1968. "Some Components of Disengagement." *Journal of Gerontology* 23:382-386.

Cooley, C. H. 1964. *Human Nature and the Social Order*. New York: Schocken.

Cumming, E., and W. Henry. 1961. *Growing Old: The Process of Disengagement*. New York: Basic Books.

Decker, D. 1980. *Social Gerontology: An Introduction to the Dynamics of Aging*. Boston: Little Brown and Company.

Desroches, F., and D. Kaiman. 1964. "Stability of Activity Participation in an Aged Population." *Journal of Gerontology* 19:211-214.

Durkheim, E. 1964. *The Division of Labor in Society*. Translated by George Simpson. New York: The Free Press.

_____. 1954. *The Elementary Forms of Religious Life*. New York: The Free Press.

_____. 1951. *Suicide*. Translated by J. A. Spaulding. Glencoe, Illinois: The Free Press.

_____. 1950. *The Rules of Sociological Method*. New York: The Free Press.
Eisenstadt, S. N. 1956. *From Generation to Generation*. Glencoe, Illinois: The Free Press.
Elliott, M. 1984. "Occupational Role Performance and Life Satisfaction in the Elderly." Master's Thesis, Department of Occupational Therapy, Medical College of Virginia, Richmond, Virginia.
Giddens, A. (Editor). 1971. *The Sociology of Suicide*. London: Frank Cass and Company, Ltd.
Graney, M. 1975. "Happiness and Social Participation in Aging." *Journal of Gerontology* 30:701-706.
Gregory, M. D. 1983. "Occupational Behavior and Life Satisfaction Among Retirees." *American Journal of Occupational Therapy* 37:548-553.
Havighurst, R. 1961. "Successful Aging." *The Gerontologist* 1:8-31.
Havighurst, R., and R. Albrecht. 1953. *Older People*. New York: Longmans.
Havighurst, R., B. Neugarten, and S. Tobin. 1968. "Disengagement and Patterns of Aging." In *Middle Age and Aging*, edited by B. Neugarten, 161-172. Chicago: University of Chicago Press.
Hochschild, A. 1975. "Disengagement Theory: A Critique and Proposal." *American Sociological Review* 40:553-569.
_____. 1973. "Community Life-Styles for the Old." *Society* 10.
Johnson, B. 1965. "Durkheim's One Cause of Suicide." *American Sociological Review* 30:875-886.
Kerns, V. 1980. "Aging and Mental Support Relations Among the Black Carib." In *Aging in Culture and Society: Comparative Viewpoints and Strategies*, edited by C. L. Fry, 112-125. New York: Bergen.
Knapp, M. 1977. "The Activity Theory of Aging: An Examination in the English Context." *Journal of Gerontology* 17:553-559.
Kutner, B., D. Fanshel, T. Langner, and A. Togo. 1956. *Five Hundred Over Sixty: A Community Survey of Aging*. New York: Russell Sage Foundation.
Lemon, B. W., V. L. Bengtson, and J. A. Peterson. 1972. "An Exploration of the Activity Theory of Aging: Activity Types and Life Satisfaction Among In-Movers to a Retirement Community." *Journal of Gerontology* 27:511-523.
Maddox, G. 1964. "Disengagement Theory: A Critical Evaluation." *The Gerontologist* 4:80-82.

_____. 1963. "Activity and Morale: A Longitudinal Study of Selected Elderly Subjects." *Social Forces* 42:195-204.

Maguire, G. H. 1983. "An Exploratory Study of the Relationship of Valued Activities to the Life Satisfaction of Elderly Persons." *Occupational Therapy Journal of Research* 3:164-172.

Maris, R. 1969. *Social Forces in Urban Suicide.* Homewood, Illinois: Dorsey Press.

McCall, G., and J. L. Simmons. 1966. *Identities and Interactions.* New York: The Free Press.

Mead, G. H. 1934. *Mind, Self, and Society.* Chicago: University of Chicago Press.

Messer, M. 1967. "The Possibility of an Age-Concentrated Environment Becoming a Normative System." *The Gerontologist* 7:247-251.

Merton, R. K. 1957. "The Role-Set: Problems in Sociological Theory." *British Journal of Sociology* 8:106-120.

Michelon, L. C. 1954. "The New Leisure Class." *American Journal of Sociology* 59:371-378.

Osgood, N. J. 1982. *Senior Settlers: Social Integration in Retirement Communities.* New York: Praeger.

Palmore, E. B. 1968. "The Effects of Aging on Activities and Attitudes." *The Gerontologist* 8:259-263.

Parsons, T. 1963. "Old Age as a Consummatory Phase." *The Gerontologist* 3:53-54.

_____. 1960. "Toward a Healthy Maturity." *Journal of Health and Human Behavior* 1:163-173.

Roman, P., and P. Taietz. 1967. "Organizational Structure and Disengagement." *The Gerontologist* 7:147-152.

Rose, A. 1964. "A Current Issue in Social Gerontology." *The Gerontologist* 4:45-50.

Rose, A., and W. Peterson (Editors). 1965. *Older People and their Social Worlds.* Philadelphia: F. A. Davis.

Rosow, I. 1967. *Social Integration of the Aged.* New York: The Free Press.

Seguin, M. M. 1973. "Opportunity for Peer Socialization in a Retirement Community." *The Gerontologist* 13:208-214.

Sheley, J. F. 1974. "Mutuality and Retirement Community Success." *International Journal of Aging and Human Development* 5:71-80.

Sherman, S. R. 1975. "Patterns of Contact for Residents of Age-Segregated and Age-Integrated Housing." *Journal of Gerontology* 30:103-107.

Sherman, S. R., W. P. Mangum, Jr., S. Dodd, R. P. Walkley, and D. M. Wilner. 1968. "Psychological Effects of Retirement Housing." *The Gerontologist* 8:170-175.

2

CREATIVITY OVER THE LIFE SPAN

INTRODUCTION AND REVIEW OF THE LITERATURE

The relationship between age and productivity was first noted by Galton in 1875. Since that time, research that has focused on the relationship between age and creativity has attempted to establish ages at which creativity peaks and declines. In 1921 Robert S. Woodworth asserted that the years from 20 to 40 are the most favorable for doing creative work of the highest order (Woodworth, 1921). Seven years after Woodworth, Nelson (1928) argued vigorously against Woodworth, citing a number of eminent individuals who did their top-notch work up to 80. This debate in the literature spurred Harvey C. Lehman to do his monumental work on creativity over the life span. His *Age and Achievement*, written in 1953, is still considered by many the definitive work on creativity over the life cycle.

In *Age and Achievement*, Lehman presented data from authoritative sources that revealed the age levels at which scientists, men of medicine, artists, scholars, writers, musicians, philosophers, leaders in business, finance, church, and politics, and technicians produced their most outstanding work or their best masterpiece. By using lists of foremost achievements compiled by experts within each field and presenting data in tabled form, plotting age against creative achievement, Lehman was able to show the peak ages of superior creative production in each field. In almost every field, except philosophy and leadership (in politics, finance, business, diplomacy, and the church), Lehman found that most superior creative achievements occur relatively early in a career, some time between the ages of 20 and 40. Lehman also established in his early study and in subsequent studies (1962, 1965) differences between peak years of production for different professions. Those in chemistry, physics, and mathematics reached their peak of productivity before or around the age of 30. Those in history and literature peaked somewhat later at 40 to 45. Philosophers and great leaders in business, church, and politics reached their peak even later, in the late 50s and early 60s. Lehman found that for most fields the rate of superior production of creative work occurred during the decade of the 30s and then gradually declined, so that about 80 percent of their superior work was completed by age 50. Lehman's findings support a decrement model of aging in which peak periods of creativity are reached early in life and then followed by accelerated and irreversible declines with aging.

Manniche and Falk (1957), who studied winners of the Nobel Peace Prize, found that most prizewinning work for chemistry and physics occurred in the 30s and for biology and medicine in the 40s. Their findings lend support to Lehman's conclusions.

Lehman's approach to the study of creativity is a product-centered one in which creativity is defined in terms of the number and quality of products produced (Kogan, 1973). Those employing a product-centered approach to the study of creativity concentrate on the physical manifestations that result from creative activity. Parnes (Parnes and Harding, 1962) best summarizes this view of creativity in the following statement:

> Creativity is that behavior which demonstrates both uniqueness and value in its product. The product may be unique and valuable to a group or organization, to society as a whole, or merely to the individual himself (p. 229).

Although well respected by many in the field, Lehman's study has been criticized by other students of creativity and aging on several grounds. Another product-centered study conducted by Wayne Dennis (1966), who studied the peak periods of creativity for 738 people who lived to age 79 or older, revealed that "the highest rate of output, in the case of nearly all groups, was reached in the forties or soon after." Dennis, unlike Lehman, was not primarily concerned with the quality of the products, but rather with the quantity produced. In his study, Dennis found that productivity remained strong through the 50s except for inventors, opera composers, and poets. Historians, philosophers, botanists, inventors, and mathematicians reached their productivity peak in the 60s; and many historians, philosophers, and scholars continued as powerful producers into their 70s. The only group that showed a decline in productivity with age was creative artists such as musicians and poets.

Other studies also present evidence that contradicts Lehman's findings. Zuckerman (1967), who studied Nobel laureates, found all of the laureates studied working productively into their 70s. Clemente and Hendricks (1973) found in their study of those receiving Ph.D.s in sociology that age at receipt of the doctorate did not significantly correlate with any of six operational indices of publication output. More recently, Simonton (1977) studied classical composers and discovered that the curve of creative productivity for these individuals followed a "backward inverted J" function. Productivity peaked in the forties and was followed by only a slight decline thereafter. These studies lead one to seriously question any conclusion that creativity declines as a function of aging.

Lehman's study has been critiqued by Dennis (1956, 1966) on several grounds. First, Dennis claims that certain deficiencies in Lehman's research design and methodology lead to a "compositional fallacy" whereby productivity of the younger years is exaggerated. Lehman did not control for differential life expectancy. By combining information pertaining to men of different degrees of longevity Lehman found higher average productivity in earlier years because to qualify for inclusion a long-lived man could have produced a significant work early or late in life, but a short-lived man could have produced a significant work only in early life. As Dennis (1956) states his argument:

> ... It seems to us that no adequate allowance can be made for the fact that all of the significant contributions of short-lived people occur in early decades, whereas the long-lived can contribute both early and late. In tabulating entries for different decades, the twenties or thirties receive a score for each short-lived person. On the other hand, the later decades, such as the sixties, contain no entries for short-lived persons and only part of the entries for septagenarians. When data from men of different degrees of longevity are included in the same table, the early decades have an inevitable loading which is not shared by the later decades (pp. 331-332).

Lehman also failed to control for different competitive structures. Dennis (1958) has argued that the apparent youthful productivity of chemists is an artifact of the fact that the number of chemists has been steadily increasing. As each chemist gets older he or she encounters more competition and thus his or her later works have less chance of achieving recognition than earlier ones. The same is true for psychologists. As Dennis (1956) points out: "Thus the best psychologist in America in 1900 was the best in a group of approximately 100. The best psychologist today, if he were ascertained, would have to be judged the best among 13,000" (p. 333).

Dennis (1956) further points out that by choosing five-year intervals extending from 20 to 70 for comparison, Lehman produced curves based on a relatively small number of entries and, as a result, several of the high values found in early age intervals result from sampling error.

As a final objection, Dennis (1956) notes that biographers and historians, who compiled the lists of "best" products from which Lehman developed his curves, may have been more likely to include a first work as the best and less likely to rate a more recent work as best because it is more difficult to rate recent contributions. Such a bias would result in more works produced in the early years being rated "best."

One other serious criticism of Lehman's study was stated by Bjorksten (1946), who suggested that as a man advances in age and attains recognition in a chosen field, he is imposed upon by increasing social, administrative, financial, and other responsibilities that take time away from creative pursuits. Based on interviews with a limited number of chemists, Bjorksten plotted a composite curve of age versus output and age versus time available for creative work. The curve reveals that the decrease in productivity with age is not due to a decline in creative capacity with age, but rather to a decline in the number of daily working hours freely available for undisturbed creative work.

Unfortunately, Chown (1977), Rabbitt (1977), and other psychologists and students of creativity and aging have interpreted the findings from Lehman's studies and other product-centered studies, which suggest declines in creative production with age, as meaning that the capacity for creativity declines with age, a very tenuous inference from data curves on creative output. Merely because an individual produces no product that is judged creative does not mean that he or she does not have the capacity for creative thinking and creative expression. As McLeish (1976) contends:

> Lehman's whole emphasis is on publications and products; but it is naive to suppose that these alone measure creativ-

ity or that ultimate break-throughs are the only criteria. One cannot say, for example, that a scientist was uncreative in his later years simply because his efforts to devise a satisfactory generalized field theory in astrophysics did not solve the enigma: he may have shown creative power in the assault without taking the bastion (p. 152).

Addressing the problem in an article in *Physics Today* (July, 1975), Lawrence Cranberg discussed the weakness of making easy generalizations about age and creativity based on identification of peak periods of production:

It is plain confusion to identify creative output, which may be readily defined in simple terms, with creativity, which is something quite different and at least as hard to define and measure as intelligence, emotional maturity, integrity, and other personality traits (Quoted in McLeish, 1976, p. 152).

The confusion of creative production with creative capacity has resulted in an unrealistic, inaccurate, overly pessimistic view of creativity and aging. Not all students of creativity take a product-centered approach. For some, the creative process or the creative person is the focus of study. Roe (1952), MacKinnon (1961), Barron (1963), Cross, Cattell, and Butcher (1967), Messick (1976) and other psychologists who take a person-centered approach to the study of creativity, are primarily interested in personality traits of creative individuals and are not particularly concerned with developmental aspects of creativity. Therefore, their work will not be reviewed here.

When we think of creativity, we usually think of novelty, originality, uniqueness, and innovative ideas. Researchers employing what Kogan (1973) calls a process-centered approach to the study of creativity, such as Getzels and Jackson (1962), Guilford (1967), Mednick (1962), and Torrance (1962) are concerned with identifying the distinctive cognitive processes involved in the production of creative products. Much of the work in this area stems from the formulation of Guilford's (1967) structure-of-intellect model that identified, through factor analysis, 64 separate intellectual abilities, some of which pertained to creative thinking dimensions.

Specific abilities such as divergent thinking (components of which include originality, spontaneous flexibility of thought, adaptive flexibility, ideational fluency, and the ability to produce transformations) and preference for complexity, which are critical to the creative process, are investigated. The components of divergent thinking identified by Guilford have been briefly defined by Alpaugh et al. (1982) as follows:

> Originality refers to either the cleverness of a response or the rarity with which it is used. Spontaneous flexibility is the ability to shift freely from one class of information to another. Adaptive flexibility is the changing of strategies or the changing--through modification or revision--of elements in terms of form and function. Ideational fluence is the speed at which appropriate ideas can be produced. Transformations are the product of a changed state due to revisions, changes, redefinitions, and modifications (pp. 102-103).

Cognitive flexibility and risk-taking are two processes that have received considerable attention and are thought to be positively correlated with creativity (Kogan, 1973; Messick, 1976).

A number of instruments have been developed to measure various aspects of the creative process. Guilford's tasks (1967) and Torrance's test of creative thinking (Torrance, 1966) are examples. Most of these instruments have been developed and used with children, adolescents, or college undergraduates (Getzels and Jackson, 1962; Davis, Peterson, and Farley, 1974).

Some researchers, who have employed a process-centered orientation, have found that the elderly, as compared with younger age groups, possess fewer abilities associated with creativity. Bromley (1956), who used the Shaw Test as a measure of creative intellectual output because it includes an exploration of abstract thinking, flexibility, originality, and fluency, found that older subjects performed at a lower level than younger subjects. He concluded that creativity declines with age. Similarly, Alpaugh and Birren (1977), who studied 111 teachers ranging in age from 20 to 83, examined the ability to think divergently, as measured by Guilford's tests (1967), and preference for complexity, as measured by the Barron-Welsh Art Scale (Barron, 1963, 1969). Age differences that favored the younger groups were found on both dimensions. Alpaugh and Birren concluded, based on their study, that: (1) there is a decline with age in divergent thinking; and (2) there is a decline, with age, in preference for complexity (p. 248). More recently, Alpaugh, Parham, Cole, and Birren (1982) examined the process of creativity and creative writing in younger and older female adults. They used Guilford's tests

(1967) to measure originality, ideational fluency, and spontaneous flexibility. Three expert raters, all of whom were English teachers at the University of Southern California, scored creative stories for creativity on a seven-point Likert Scale. Both quantitative and qualitative differences in creativity by age were observed. All differences were in favor of younger subjects. Older individuals were less creative than younger individuals, both as measured by their performance on Guilford's tests and as judged by experts on the creative writing exercise. It is noteworthy, however, that the second highest score on creativity was obtained by the oldest subject, who was 83.

One must interpret findings from these studies with caution. Several methodological problems, which will be discussed in this section, plague the studies and seriously limit their conclusions regarding the relationship between creativity and aging.

The studies reviewed used a cross-sectional research design to demonstrate a decline in creativity with age. Major studies conducted recently on the relationship between another cognitive ability, intelligence, and age using sequential strategies of analysis, in which it is possible to separate cohort or generational effects from age effects, have found that the major proportion of age differences can be explained by cohort variations (Schaie, 1977; Schaie and Labouvie-Vief, 1974; Schaie and Strother, 1968). As Schaie and Labouvie-Vief (1974) point out regarding earlier research which supported the decrement model of cognitive functions in adulthood:

> But recently researchers turned toward a discussion of the intricate relationship between ontogenetic and historical (generational) change (e.g., Kuhlen, 1963; Riegel and Riegel, 1972; Schaie, 1965, 1970, 1972, 1973) the validity of this finding has been seriously challenged. That is, since the typical cross-sectional study samples groups of individuals not only differing in age, but also originating from widely varying environmental backgrounds, the resulting age-performance functions can rarely be taken as indicators of ontogenetic patterns (p. 305).

Based on their well-known and well-respected analyses of intellectual abilities and age, in which they combined a series of cross-sectional and longitudinal studies in complex sequential designs, which allowed them to differentiate between age effects on the one hand and generation-related differences on the other, Schaie and Labouvie-Vief (1974) concluded:

> . . . Concentrating on the generation confound existing in
> conventional cross-sectional research, the data reported
> here lend minimal justification to the often stated stereo-
> type of general behavioral deficit in late adulthood and
> maybe old age--a finding that, incidentally, is supported
> by recent longitudinal data suggesting that decrements may
> occur only in the years immediately preceding death. . . .
> Similarly, genuine longitudinal decline exists only for a
> few of the cognitive dimensions included in this study.
> Our knowledge of life-span changes in intellectual ontoge-
> ny, therefore, requires a much more explicit focus on the
> application of methodologies aimed at differentiating onto-
> genetic and cultural change components (p. 319).

Because age and cohort are confounded in the cross-sectional studies just reviewed, it is impossible to know whether the observed decrements in creativity are really due to maturational changes or to generational differences. For example, different cohorts may have been exposed to different types of educational environments and learning materials and experiences, as well as different sociocultural events that might affect their performance on creativity measures. Different external criteria of creativity may be appropriate for different age and cohort groups. As Kogan (1973) so aptly notes, cohort groups whose peak productive years coincide with an innovative surge in the field will obviously have a greater opportunity for creative accomplishment; and in fields experiencing rapid change, age-based declines in creativity may actually simply reflect the emergence of new cohorts representing the "new wave" (p. 158).

The studies also suffer from other methodological problems, which lead one to question their validity and reliability. As was pointed out earlier, the instruments used to measure creativity were developed for and used with younger age populations such as children and college undergraduates. These instruments may not be appropriate or valid when used with older individuals (Romaniuk, 1978). The important question as posed by Romaniuk and Romaniuk (1981) in their article entitled "Creativity Across the Life Span: A Measurement Perspective" is: "Are measures of creativity derived from one age and cohort group valid when applied to others?" (p. 371) A test may also have different meanings for different age and cohort groups tested, which raises the serious issues of equivalence (Labouvie, 1979) and construct validity (Romaniuk and Romaniuk, 1981).

Not only is the validity of the instruments used to measure creativity in question, but the reliability of the measures and the assessment process may also be limited. As Starkweather (1968) reminds us, assessment conditions and measurement procedures, which emphasize timed performance, large numbers of items with standard response requirements, and standardized directions and scoring procedures, may not reliably tap the creative process and may favor the young over the old. As Romaniuk and Romaniuk (1981) caution:

> Age and cohort groups may differ in their experience and approach to the testing situation which may influence performance on creativity measures. For instance, there may be important differences in test sophistication, test anxiety, motivation, or test conceptualizations between retirees, college students, and children which could influence their test results independent of creative ability (p. 373).

In fact, a large body of gerontological literature supports the fact that the elderly do poorly in test situations, especially when they are timed and evaluated and when they must make quick decisions or take risks to succeed. Welford (1958) demonstrated that the elderly react poorly under timed pressure, are highly sensitive to being evaluated under test conditions, and often manifest symptoms of withdrawal from assessment situations. Similarly, Botwinick (1973) has found that older subjects may be inappropriately and overly aroused in experimental situations, thus impairing their performance. There is also evidence that older individuals tend to be more cautious than younger individuals. Canestrari (1963) found that older subjects tended to make more errors of omission than errors of commission; and Botwinick (1973) discovered that, when presented with examples of life situations involving risks, older people expressed a desire not to act at all. The cautiousness and fear of taking risks, which has been shown to be more characteristic of older individuals than of younger persons, might have a major affect on cognitive flexibility and risk-taking, two cognitive dimensions associated with the creative process. Also, the unwillingness to risk being wrong, which results in no response on the part of the elderly subject, greatly restricts fluency of ideas, which is a very important component of divergent thinking. These studies also suggest that the elderly shy away from ambiguous situations, which is not very conducive to creativity. Birren (1964) explains that the elderly prefer not to deal with complexity and shy away from ambiguity because with increasing age there appears to be increased reliance on cognitive and affective "load shedding."

We have some evidence to suggest that, if some of the constraints associated with the testing situation could be lessened or removed, older individuals would perform better. Arenberg (1973) and Eisdorfer (1965) have effectively demonstrated that self-pacing and increased time of exposure to stimulus materials in learning experiments, what they called an "optimal" context for the elderly, resulted in improved performance among elderly subjects. Similarly, Klein and Birren (1973) were able to reduce the tendency toward conformity by raising the level of self-perceived competence of elderly subjects. There is strong evidence to indicate that even when the time factor is held constant, changes in ideational productivity and uniqueness vary according to whether test-like or game-like assessment conditions prevail (Kogan and Morgan, 1969; Nicholls, 1971).

The supposed decline with age of creativity might simply reflect cautiousness, fear of taking risks, and inability to perform well on structured tests under timed conditions, all of which are characteristic of the elderly. The pessimistic picture of decrement may be exaggerated or unwarranted.

Romaniuk and Romaniuk (1981) note two other threats to reliability. Interjudge and intrajudge variability may threaten reliability because most tests of creative ability are scored by individuals. Bias in the initial selection of scoring criteria and potential changes in selection criteria over time may also threaten reliability of measures across different age groups or cohorts.

All of the studies reviewed suffer from one other major problem: age may not be the explanatory variable, but rather just an index of other factors that are really responsible for the decline in creativity over the life cycle. Lehman (1962), Kogan (1973), Butler (1967), and others have suggested that age-correlated physical, psychological, and social factors may account for decline in creativity with age. It takes energy to be creative (Troll, 1982; Stevens-Long, 1979); and Birren (1964) and others have demonstrated that older people often have less energy to deal with their environment than do younger individuals. Reduce energy, pain and illness, poverty, malnutrition, ageism, discrimination, and negative self-images, declining sensory capacities, and changes in motivation, all correlated with age, may set a limit on an individual's creative accomplishments, but not on his or her capacity for creativity.

Even Lehman (1962) has admitted that age itself may not cause declines in creativity but rather may be an index of other variables that are responsible for the decline. As he writes:

> Although I would be happy to be able to state the specific causes of age differences in production rates, the mere fact that I have assembled some statistics is no indication that I know any more with reference to cause-and-effect relationships than does the reader. The age factor of itself could hardly be regarded as causing anything at all. It is the concomitants of advancing age that need to be examined . . . a decrement in physical vigor and sensory capacity, more illness, glandular changes, more preoccupation with practical concerns, less favorable conditions for concentration, weakened intellectual curiosity, more mental disorders and an accumulation of unfavorable habits. . . . Moreover, the individual who has achieved prestige and recognition may try less hard thereafter to achieve further success (p. 416).

Robert Butler (1967), in reporting on the studies of human aging conducted at the National Institute of Mental Health at Bethesda, Maryland, from 1955 to 1962, stresses the extent to which factors other than aging affect the experience and characteristics of aging. These studies revealed, for example, that cerebral blood flow and oxygen consumption did *not* decrease as a function of aging *per se*, as is commonly supposed. Rather, when such changes did occur, they were the result of arteriosclerosis. These studies also showed that performance on psychometric tests was not affected by aging; however, the presence of disease strongly affected performance. These studies further revealed that health status, arterial blood pressure, depression, and environmental deficits had a major influence on both mean reaction time and general speed. Disease, not aging *per se*, explained several manifestations commonly thought to be associated with aging. Socioeconomic conditions, cultural attitudes, and personality also influenced behavior. A broad conclusion from these studies may be stated as follows:

> As a consequence of an intensive and extensive multidisciplinary study, the investigators found evidence to suggest that many manifestations heretofore associated with aging per se reflect instead medical illness, personality variables, and sociocultural effects. This result would not surprise

such observers as Zeman (1957), who has written of the tendency in the past to blame many obscure conditions on "old age" (Butler, 1967, p. 27).

The problem of the status of age as a variable in developmental research may have contributed to the pessimistic view of creativity over the life span. As Romaniuk and Romaniuk (1981) suggest in their illustration: "Arthritic hands, declining stamina, and failing eyesight, for example, may impede an older painter's productivity, but have no effect on the artist's capacity to conceptualize unique relationships in the world" (p. 368).

The few studies reviewed in this chapter represent the bulk of the work on creativity over the life cycle. As this review suggests, we currently have painfully few studies of creativity and aging, especially as compared to the volume of research on intelligence and aging. We are left with a variety of different definitions of creativity, a lack of information on creativity and aging, contradictory findings on the relationship between age and creativity, and several studies whose findings must be questioned in light of their methodological limitations and problems in interpretation. In light of all these problems and existing gaps in the empirical literature, it is very important that we seriously question the existing pessimistic view of aging and creativity and realize that perhaps the old remain just as creative as the young. In fact, creativity may even be enhanced as one ages and experiences an abundance of nonstructured, noncommitted, "free" time to think and to relax and to dream. It is just possible that a wealth of experience, skills, and knowledge, only obtained over a lifetime of living, is a necessary ingredient for creative expression. If so, then the elderly certainly have an advantage over the young.

Some psychologists and theorists in the field have refused to accept the decrement model of creativity and aging presented in some of the empirical studies just reviewed. Instead, they have conceptualized creativity as a lifelong process, although sometimes manifested differently at different stages of life. These theories and conceptualizations will be reviewed in the following section of this chapter.

THEORETICAL/CONCEPTUAL MODELS

The theoretical literature on creativity and aging, although quite sparse, has attempted to identify qualities and aspects of creativity over the life cycle with particular emphasis on characteristics of the creative older person. From tape recorded oral histories and interviews that he has collected from older individuals since 1962, Butler (1974) has described general personality characteristics of creative individuals. From his work with oral history tapes and interviews, as well as his reading of autobiographies and memoirs written by older individuals who have remained creative into their later years, Butler has concluded that there is an "autodidactic" character to the creative personality; and this character remains present throughout life (Butler, 1967, 1974). As Butler (1974) describes the autodidact:

> The autodidact operates in some unusual ways. He is literally a self-teacher. His central focus is upon the self--an essential belief in the self, an exploitation of it, and the effort to exhaust all of its possibilities. The autodidact tries to learn everything for himself; he teaches himself what he already knows and what others have found out, and in the process uncovers or creates what only he can teach--that is something "new" (p. 97).

Henri Rosseau taught himself to paint. Benjamin Franklin, totally self-educated, taught himself, among other things, five languages, algebra, and geometry. Rosseau and Franklin were autodidacts, to use Butler's term. So were George Bernard Shaw, Alexis Emmanuel Chabrier, Grandma Moses, Edward Gibbon, and Charles Darwin. These individuals continued learning throughout their lives. One characteristic that distinguishes the autodidact from others is that he or she never accepts a fact or truth that others consider self-evident; instead, the autodidact questions, searches for new answers, studies more to be sure, reflects more comprehensively. "Never satisfied with what is known, the autodidact pushes onward in an ever unfolding adventure of the self" (Williamson, Evans, and Munley, 1980, p. 85). According to Butler, autodidacticism may be an essential ingredient for creativity at any age.

Similar to the notion of the autodidact is the concept of the "Ulyssean Adult" put forth by McLeish (1976), in which he describes the personality characteristics of people who develop or maintain creative activity in the later years. Some Ulyssean adults, such as Grandma Moses, may experience the first surge of creativity in late life. These individuals McLeish terms Ulyssean Ones. For others, like Pablo Picasso or Bertrand Russell, creativity may have been a life-long companion that manifests itself in a variety of ways throughout life. These individuals McLeish refers to as Ulyssean Twos. In his description of the Ulyssean adult, McLeish (1976) writes:

> These Ulyssean people have one thing in common--they are all seekers, and this is reflected in the trajectory of their lives. Some are chiefly thinkers and readers, adventurers in ideas, some chiefly doers, many are both; all are in pursuit of new enterprises for the mind, the body, or the spirit. The scale of the enterprises, whether large or small, is incidental; the symbol of the Ulyssean is the prow of the ship in which Ulysses and his comrades had so many encounters on the swift-running seas. The thrust is outward--ever inquiring, searching, dreaming, growing--outward not downward (p. 155).

One adult educator, Cyril Houle (1961), who was fascinated by one particular group of learners--the learning-oriented adult learner who takes courses and studies because he or she loves to pursue knowledge "for its own sake"--described these individuals by the phrase *cacoethes studendi* ("the itch to learn").

The Ulyssean is an adventurer who treats life as an exciting journey from beginning to end. He or she faces each day with a sense of wonder and awe, a searching spirit, openness to adventure and new experiences, and a willingness to be creative. As McLeish (1976) puts it, the Ulyssean adult believes in the Second Chance, and the Third, and the Fourth. He or she is not afraid to try new and different things even late in life, just as Ulysses did when he began his last set of adventures described in *The Odyssey* at about age 70. According to McLeish (1976), some of the other qualities that especially identify the Ulyssean person in late life include: a sense of quest, courage, resourcefulness, creativity, and the quality of intense humanness or being a "real" person. The Ulyssean adult, as described by McLeish, resembles Maslow's (1968) self-actualized individual.

In developing his concept of the Ulyssean adult, McLeish was quick to point out that the Ulyssean life is possible for older individuals because in many ways the conditions required for the creative life are more available in the later years of adulthood than earlier in life. Older individuals have more time to rest and to think; they also possess a rich storehouse of experiences accumulated through a lifetime, which are recorded in the apparatus of the mind; and older individuals are more free to adapt unorthodox concepts, and unorthodoxy is one of the recognized patterns of creativity (1976, pp. 246-247).

Other students of creativity and aging have identified different types or stages of creativity that emerge at different points over the life course. Lehman (1953) first suggested that different types of creativity characterize different life stages. He found, for example, that the creativity of science and invention, which requires fresh new ideas or perspectives, characterizes young adulthood; whereas, the creative in philosophy and leadership, which requires an accumulation of knowledge and experience over time, is more characteristic of late life.

Butler (1967, 1974) has also identified qualitative and quantitative changes in creativity over the life cycle. His characteristic mode lifecycle theory, based upon and derived from interview data collected while he was at the Washington School of Psychiatry, suggests that certain types of creativity are more characteristic of late life than are others, most notably: comprehensive reconstructions of a lifetime of scholarship; study and reflection; revision, reconsideration, and retraction; continuing development of material; concern with aging and the life cycle, geriatrics, or gerontology; and composing memoirs (Butler, 1967, pp. 35-37).

As Lehman (1953) noted in his early work, "the old usually possess greater wisdom and erudition" (Quoted in Butler, 1967, p. 37). Building upon this important observation, Butler (1967) suggests that creative products in late life differ from those of earlier years. Comprehensive reconstructions of a lifetime of scholarship, study, and reflection, for instance, are only possible in late life after a great deal of living and learning has occurred. Some late life capacities that influence the nature and type of creativity expressed at this stage include: accumulated knowledge and skills, judgment, wisdom and understanding, patience and prudence, candor, maturity, and serenity, contentment, and calm. As Butler (1967) also remarks:

> The absence of so-called new ideas or new forms is not a test of creativity per se, because one's mode of being, one's past interests, training, skills, and experience, may be creatively elaborated and extended. Although first and highly significant creative works are likely to be produced in early years (20-35), the fact that other "new directions" do not occur is not equivalent to declining creativity (p. 39).

Echoing the views of Butler, Jacques (1964) speaks of "hot-from-the-fire" creativity of young adulthood and "sculpted" creativity of mid-life. The prototypes of the intense, spontaneous, "hot-from-the-fire" creativity of youth are Mozart and Keats.

Shakespeare and Dickens are prototypes of the more "sculpted" creativity of mid-life, which requires experience, revision, and reflection.

Based on his research at the Center for Creative Leadership, Irving Taylor (1974) has developed a model of creativity that attempts to examine creativity from a life-cycle developmental perspective. In his stage model of creativity, Taylor conceptualizes different types and forms of creative expressions that seem to develop in and have their roots in different stages of the life cycle. The five sequential stages of creativity, which are associated with different types of creative expression across the life span, are: (1) expressive spontaneity, found in spontaneous drawings of children, free athletic games, extemporaneous dance, and impromptu language, which occurs from the earliest years to approximately six; (2) technical proficiency, in which continuous refinement and training is encouraged, largely from external sources, which occurs from six until adolescence; (3) inventive ingenuity, which takes the forms of idealized drawings, gadgetry, and general tinkering with materials, which is characteristic of adolescence through the early 20s; (4) innovative flexibility, or adaptability that results in modification of basic ideas, systems, and organizations made earlier, which is characteristic of the 20s and 30s; and (5) emergentive originality, the final form of creativity, which is the disposition to create original and essentially new ideas and seems to flourish in the late 50s and into the 60s, 70s, 80s, and 90s (pp. 113-114). Based on his studies with individuals of different ages, Taylor (1974) concluded:

> The implications of the above concepts and supportive research are that creativity need not necessarily decline with age, but may change its form toward a deeper and more basic form of creativity during later years when the person seeks fundamental and basic ideas either in his own life style or in the field in which he is involved (p. 116).

Taylor's findings support earlier findings of Haefele (1962), Stern (1967), Buhler (1968), Butler (1967, 1974), McLeish (1976), and others who have suggested that creativity continues throughout one's life span.

In the next section we will examine the lives of some older individuals to shed further light on the issue of creativity and aging.

EXAMPLES OF CREATIVE SENIORS

As the previous discussion indicates, we presently possess very few reliable scientific studies of creativity over the life span; and what few studies do exist are contradictory, and several suffer from conceptual or methodological problems. Many of these studies, which would lead us to accept the decrement model and conclude that creativity declines with age, confuse creative capacity with creative productivity. Some individuals working in the area, however, do not accept these findings. Those describing the autodidactic or the Ulyssean adult suggest that creativity does not stop at any age, but rather continues throughout the life course, as long as serious illness or health problems, malnutrition, extreme poverty, or some of the other external conditions related to the aging process are held in check. Another way we might gain a glimpse of the true story of creativity in late life is to look at the lives of some well-known elderly individuals. When the student of human behavior embarks upon the search for individuals who retain their creative capacities into the latest years of life, he or she soon discovers many remarkable examples of creative oldsters. In this section we will be looking at the lives of some older individuals who continued to produce creatively in the areas of art, music, drama, science, politics, and peace until they died.

In the field of music among the many creative older composers, conductors, and performers some of the most noteworthy include: Johann Sebastian Bach, regarded as one of the greatest of all composers, who continued to produce music into his mid-60s, making one of his most famous masterpieces, *Mass in B Minor* at the age of 59 and coining the musical techniques of *fugue* and *counterpoint* during the later years of his life; Giuseppe Verdi, Italy's greatest nineteenth-century composer, who wrote two of his finest operas, *Otello* and *Falstaff*, in his 80s and completed his *Stabat Mater* at 84; Arthur Rubenstein, who at 80 was playing piano better than at any time previously; César Auguste Franck, who composed his famous *Symphony in D Minor* between 64 and 66; Claudio Monteverdi, an Italian composer of the 1600s, best known for his operas and eight books of madrigals, the eighth of which was published when he was 71; Arthur Fiedler, the well-known conductor of the Boston Pops who conducted into his 90s; Leonard Bernstein, who has composed works for orchestra and piano, ballet, choral pieces and chamber music, and scores for theatre--including the musical score for *Peter Pan*, *Candide*, and *West Side Story*--conducted the New York Philharmonic Orchestra, and today at 68 shows no signs of modifying his high-paced creative life of musical composing and world-wide performances; and Leopold Stokowski, a central figure in the musical life of the United States for more than half a century, who organized the All-American Youth Orchestra at age 59 and the American Symphony for gifted, talented youngsters at age 79.

Writing plays, poetry, novels, fiction, and philosophy are major creative endeavors. A look at the lives of some of the most famous writers reveals that many individuals remain productive and creative into their later years. Some of the more well-known creative writers who have continued to produce creative work into their later years include: Sophocles, classical Greek playwright who wrote *Oedipus Rex* at 75; John Milton and William Butler Yeats, writers who produced some of their best work in late life; Bertrand Russell, philosopher and defender of liberty, who received the Nobel Prize for Literature at 78; Spanish writer, Cervantes, who produced his masterpiece, *Don Quixote de la Mancha*, from 58 to 68; Goethe, who wrote *Faust* in his 80s; Tolstoy, who completed *What is Art?* at 88; Carl Sandburg, the well-known poet, who at 70 wrote his first novel, *Remembrance Rock*; Santayana, well-known philosopher, who wrote his first novel, *The Last Puritan*, when he was 72; William F. De Morgan, who in his early life was an inventor and designed glass and tiles and who wrote his first novel, *Joseph Vance*, at 65 and continued to write approximately one novel a year for the next 11 years he lived; and Sigmund Freud, outspoken critic of continuing creativity in the later years, who nevertheless himself wrote *The Ego and the Id* at 67 and *Analysis Terminable and Interminable* at 81.

One of the most famous U.S. poets of all time, Robert Frost, began publishing poetry at age 15 and continued to publish into his later years, receiving the Pulitzer Prize four times, the last time at age 69 for *A Witness Tree*.

Producing a beautiful painting or piece of sculpture or designing a building is truly a creative endeavor. Many well-known artists and architects have produced their greatest masterpieces in the later years of life. Some of the more well-known artists who have made major contributions in late life include: Claude Monet, French Impressionist painter who completed his famous lily paintings in his later years; Rembrandt, who continued to paint self-portraits into his 70s; Titian, who painted some of his best works in his 70s, completing *The Battle of Lepanto* at age 98, and continuing to paint until his death at 99; Tintoretto, who completed his famous *Fall of the Mahha* at 76; Franz Hals, who completed *The Governors of the Almshouse* at 84; Michelangelo, High

Renaissance sculptor, architect, painter, and poet, who became chief architect at St. Peter's Church in Rome at age 72 and who completed some of his most important work in painting and poetry between 70 and 89, including frescoing the Pauline Chapel; Frank Lloyd Wright, great U.S. architect, who at 91 completed the Guggenheim Museum; and the United States' favorite grandmother, Grandma Moses, who began painting at 76 and who continued producing her well-known paintings until she died at 101.

No account of creativity would be complete without offering examples of actors and actresses who have remained active and creative into the later years. Recalling famous actors and actresses who have contributed much in their later years, the following names come to mind: Bette Davis, Ethel Barrymore, Katharine Hepburn, Henry Fonda, Bob Hope, John Wayne, Bing Crosby, and George Burns.

Creativity involves the creation and production of something new; and scientific invention and developments in mathematics represent high forms of creative expression. Several well-known scientific inventors and mathematicians have made major contributions in their later years. Zuckerman (1967), who studied the patterns of productivity of Nobel Laureates in science, found that all nine of the laureates continued to publish beyond the age of 70. The oldest one still at work was over 80. Notable scientists and mathematicians who continued creatively into their later years include Albert Einstein, who was still doing productive work and writing on different branches and developments from the Theory of Relativity and lecturing well into his 70s; Marie Curie, twice awarded the Nobel Prize for Chemistry for her discovery of and work with radium, who was actively researching and was writing the best of all her books, *Radioactivity*, when she died at 67; Friedrich Heinrich von Humboldt, author of *Kosmos*, one of the world's greatest scientific achievements (in which the known facts of the universe are formulated), who published the volumes between 76 and 91; Benjamin Duggar, who after he was arbitrarily retired from his university professorship at the age of 72, discovered aureomycin and chlortetracycline, an antibiotic; Pierre Joseph Van Bennder, who at 74 began the study of the early history of the animal egg and discovered that chromosomes have a genetic continuity throughout the life cycle; Galileo Gallilei, who at 72 published *Dialoghi delle Nuave Scienze* in which he recapitulated results of his earlier experiments and offered mature meditations on the principles of mechanics; and Thomas Edison, who worked on improving technology and industrializing the use of electricity and made countless contributions that helped revolutionize our world, from the electric light bulb to the microphone and phonograph, and who took up the serious study of botany at the age of 80, testing over 17,000 different plants to find a domestic source of natural rubber.

Creative individuals are found not only in music, the arts, and science, but also in politics and peace. Golda Meir, the Jewish girl of Russian descent who devoted her life to the cause of Jews, creating a place in Palestine where all Jews could find freedom, served as Prime Minister of Israel through two Middle East wars until she was 75. She continued to work up to 20 hours a day in her 70s, striving for peace and building a strong nation. Mother Theresa of Calcutta, winner of the Nobel Peace Prize in 1979 for her charitable work with the poor in India where she established the Ministries of Charity and worked with lepers, the destitute, and the dying, is still laboring hard for the poor at age 74. Her work has spread across four continents. Mahatma Gandhi, India's great statesman and spiritual leader, was an elder who influenced the lives of millions in India and around the world.

Of course, not all elderly individuals have the genius of autodidacts or Ulysseans such as Pablo Picasso, George Bernard Shaw, or Benjamin Franklin; but most aging persons have some capacity for creative expression. As McLeish (1976) so appropriately states the case in *The Ulyssean Adult*:

> Meanwhile, where are the records of creative action of those remarkable people, the later adults whose names are not found in "celebrated lists"; who in their late 50's, 60's, and 70's, and far older cannot turn off their minds; who remain entranced by the wonder of the world; and whose later years make a mockery of the claim that the curve of the life journey is a simple hill with a summit at age 50 and a progressive decline thereafter? Who plots the curves of the lives of these creators who creativity extends to dozens of domains in arts, sciences, politics, and invention? (pp. 154-155).

Creativity is not always and only manifest through the arts, science, invention, or politics. Creatively meeting the day-to-day tasks of life in our complex society is a form of creativity, which is evident in the lives of many elderly individuals whose names do not appear in any *Who's Who*. As Anderson (1959) points out, there is another kind of creativity, which he terms "psychological or social invention," which suggests creativity in human relations. Arranging car pools, keeping on good terms with neighbors, making love, and child-rearing are examples. The elderly have many of the necessary qualities for creativity: time, accumulated experience, knowledge, skills, and wisdom. The Bible emphasized wisdom as a quality of the old. Similarly, Eastern philosophies stress continued opportunities for growth in knowledge, experience, and wisdom in late life.

As the literature review presented earlier reveals, we presently have few studies of creativity in late life and even fewer that have investigated the conditions and environmental factors that enhance or inhibit creative expression in late life. Romaniuk (1982) has conducted creative thinking workshops with older individuals with some success. Birren (1979) has had success with a class designed to facilitate the writing of a creative life review by presenting topics for short essays such as "The History of My Relationships" and "Branching Points in My Life" (Alpaugh et al., 1982, p. 115). Literature reviewed previously also indicates that providing a non-pressured environment, free of anxiety and time constraints, in which the elderly individuals feel safe and good about themselves, enhances creativity among older individuals. Certain aspects of creativity, which may be nurtured and developed by taking special environmental conditions into account, have been referred to as the "teachable" aspects of creativity.

We can also stimulate creativity and allow the elderly to develop and use their I.Q. ("imagination quotient") (Polansky, 1974) by providing enriching environments and experiences through art, drama, music, and dance. Involvement in these creative activities stimulates the senses and invigorates the body and mind.

REFERENCES

Alpaugh, P. K., and J. E. Birren. 1977. "Variables Affecting Creative Contributions Across the Adult Life Span." *Human Development* 20:240-248.

Alpaugh, P. K., I. Parham, K. D. Cole, and J. E. Birren. 1982. "Creativity in Adulthood and Old Age: An Exploratory Study." *Educational Gerontology* 8:101-116.

Alpaugh, P. K., V. J. Renner, and J. E. Birren. 1976. "Age and Creativity: Implications for Education and Teachers." *Educational Gerontology* 1:17-40.

Anderson, H. H. 1959. "Creativity in Perspective." In *Creativity and Its Cultivation*, edited by H. H. Anderson. New York: Harper and Brothers.

Arenberg, D. 1973. "Cognition and Aging: Verbal Learning, Memory, Problem Solving, and Aging." In *The Psychology of Adult Development and Aging*, edited by C. Eisdorfer and M. P. Lawton, pp. 74-97. Washington, D.C.: American Psychological Association.

Barron, F. 1969. *Creative Person and Creative Process*. New York: Holt.

_____. 1963. *Creativity and Psychological Health*. New York: Van Nostrand.

Birren, J. E. 1979. Personal communication referred to in Alpaugh, P. K., Parham, I., K. D. Cole, and J. E. Birren. "Creativity in Adulthood and Old Age: An Exploratory Study." *Educational Gerontology* 8:115.

_____. 1964. *The Psychology of Aging*. Englewood Cliffs, New Jersey: Prentice-Hall.

Bjorksten, J. 1946. "The Limitation of Creative Years." *Scientific Monthly* 62:94.

Botwinick, J. 1973. *Aging and Behavior*. New York: Springer.

Bromley, D. B. 1956. "Some Experimental Tests of the Effect of Age on Creative Intellectual Output." *Journal of Gerontology* 11:74-82.

Buhler, C. 1968. "The General Structure of the Human Life Cycle." In *The Course of Human Life*, edited by C. Buhler and F. Massarik. New York: Springer.

Butler, R. N. 1974. "The Creative Life and Old Age." In *Successful Aging*, edited by E. Pfeiffer, pp. 97-108. Durham, North Carolina: Duke University Study of Aging and Human Development.

_____. 1967. "The Destiny of Creativity in Later Life: Studies of Creative People and the Creative Process." In *Psychodynamic Studies on Aging*, edited by S. Levin and R. J. Kahana, pp. 20-63. New York: International Universities Press.

Canestrari, R. E., Jr. 1963. "Paced and Self-Paced Learning in Young and Elderly Adults." *Journal of Gerontology* 18:165-168.

Chown, S. 1977. "Morale, Careers, and Personal Potentials." In *The Psychology of Aging*, pp. 672-691, edited by J. Birren and K. W. Schaie. New York: Van Nostrand and Reinhold.

Clemente, F., and J. Hendricks. 1973. "A Further Look at the Relationship Between Age and Productivity." *The Gerontologist* 13: 106-110.

Comfort, A. 1976. *A Good Age*. New York: Simon and Schuster.

Cross, P., R. B. Cattell, and H. J. Butcher. 1967. "The Personality Pattern of Creative Artists." *British Journal of Educational Psychology* 37:292-299.

Dangott, L., and R. Kalish. 1979. *A Time to Enjoy the Pleasures of Aging*. Englewood Cliffs, New Jersey: Prentice-Hall.

Davis, G. A., J. M. Peterson, and F. H. Farley. 1974. "Attitudes, Motivation, Sensation Seeking and Belief in ESP, as Predictors of Real Creative Behavior." *Journal of Creative Behavior* 8:31-39.

Dennis, W. 1966. "Creative Productivity Between the Ages of 20 and 80 Years." *Journal of Gerontology* 21:1-8.

_____. 1958. "The Age Decrement in Outstanding Scientific Contributions: Fact or Artifact?" *American Psychologist* 13:457-460.

_____. 1956. "Age and Achievement: A Critique." *Journal of Gerontology* 11:331-333.

Eisdorfer, C. 1965. "Verbal Learning Response Time in the Aged." *Journal of Genetic Psychology* 107:15-22.

Galton, F. 1875. "Twins as a Criterion of the Relative Power of Nature and Nurture." *Journal of the Royal Anthropological Institute* 5:324-329.

Getzels, J. W., and P. W. Jackson. 1962. *Creativity and Intelligence: Explorations with Gifted Students*. New York: Wiley.

Guilford, J. P. 1967. *The Nature of Human Intelligence*. New York: McGraw-Hill.

Haefele, J. W. 1962. *Creativity and Innovation*. New York: Reinhold.

Houle, C. 1961. *The Inquiring Mind*. Madison, Wisconsin: University of Wisconsin Press.

Jacques, E. 1964. "Death and the Mid-Life Crisis." *International Journal of Psychoanalysis* 46:502-514.

Klein, R. L., and J. E. Birren. 1973. *Age, Perceived Self-Competency, and Conformity*. Proceedings of the 81st Annual Convention of the American Psychological Association (APA): pp. 779-780. Washington, D.C.: APA.

Kogan, N. 1973. "Creativity and Cognitive Style: A Life-Span Perspective." In *Life-Span Developmental Psychology Personality and Socialization*, edited by P. B. Baltes and K. W. Schaie, pp. 145-161. New York: Academic Press.

Kogan, N., and F. T. Morgan. 1969. "Task and Motivational Influences on the Assessment of Creative and Intellective Ability in Children." *Genetic Psychology Monographs* 80:91-127.

Kuhlen, R. G. 1963. *Psychological Backgrounds of Adult Education.* Chicago: CSLEA.

Labouvie, E. W. 1979. "Identity vs. Equivalence of Psychological Measures and Constructs." Paper presented at the Annual Meetings of the American Psychological Association New York, New York.

Lehman, H. C. 1966. "The Psychologist's Most Creative Years." *Psychology* 21:363-369.

_____. 1965. "The Production of Masters' Works Prior to Age 30." *The Gerontologist* 5:24-30.

_____. 1962. "The Creative Production Rates of Present Versus Past Generations of Scientists." *Journal of Gerontology* 17:409-417.

_____. 1953. *Age and Achievement.* Princeton, New Jersey: Princeton University Press.

MacKinnon, D. W. 1961. "The Personality Correlates of Creativity: A Study of American Architects." In *Proceedings of the XIV International Congress of Applied Psychology,* edited by G. S. Nielson, pp. 11-39. Copenhagen: Munks-Gaared.

Manniche, E., and G. Falk. 1957. "Age and the Nobel Prize." *Behavior Science* 2:301-307.

Maslow, A. H. 1968. *Toward a Psychology of Being.* New York: Van Nostrand and Reinhold.

McLeish, J. 1976. *The Ulyssean Adult.* Toronto: McGraw-Hill.

Mednick, S. A. 1962. "The Associative Basis of the Creative Process." *Psychological Review* 69:220-232.

Messick, S. 1976. "Personality Consistencies in Cognition and Creativity." In *Individuality in Learning,* edited by S. Messick, et al. San Francisco: Jossey-Bass.

Nelson, H. 1928. "The Creative Years." *American Journal of Psychology* 40:303-311.

Nicholls, J. G. 1971. "Some Effects of Testing Procedure on Divergent Thinking." *Child Development* 42:1647-1651.

O'Brian, P. 1976. *Pablo Ruiz Picasso: A Biography.* London: Collins.

Parnes, S. J., and H. F. Harding (Editors). 1962. *A Source Book for Creative Thinking.* New York: Scribners.

Polansky, G. 1974. "Age and Creativity." In *Successful Aging: A Conference Report,* edited by E. Pfeiffer, pp. 109-111. Durham, North Carolina: Duke University Press.

Rabbitt, P. 1977. "Changes in Problem Solving Ability in Old Age." In *The Psychology of Aging,* edited by J. Birren and K. W. Schaie, pp. 606-625. New York: Van Nostrand and Reinhold.

Riegel, K., and Riegel, R. 1972. "Development, Drop, and Death." *Developmental Psychology* 6:306-319.

Roe, A. A. 1952. "A Psychologist Examines Sixty-Four Eminent Scientists." *Scientific American* 187:21-25.

Romaniuk, J. G. 1982. "Creative Thinking Workshops." *Lifelong Learning: The Adult Years* May:12-15.

_____. 1978. *Training Creativity in the Elderly: An Examination of Attitudes, Self-Perceptions, and Abilities.* Unpublished doctoral dissertation, Madison, Wisconsin, University of Wisconsin--Madison.

Romaniuk, J., and M. Romaniuk. 1981. "Creativity Across the Life Span: A Measurement Perspective." *Human Development* 24:366-381.

Schaie, K. W. 1977. "Quasi-Experimental Research Designs." In *Handbook of the Psychology of Aging*, edited by J. Birren and K. W. Schaie, pp. 39-58. New York: Van Nostrand and Reinhold.

_____. 1973. "Methodological Problems in Descriptive Developmental Research on Adulthood and Aging." In *Life-Span Developmental Psychology*, pp. 253-279, edited by J. R. Nesselroade and A. W. Reese. New York: Academic Press.

_____. 1972. "Limitations on the Generalizability of Growth Curves on Intelligence." *Human Development* 15:141-152.

_____. 1970. "A Reinterpretation of Age Related Changes in Cognitive Structure and Functioning." In *Life-Span Developmental Psychology*, edited by L. Goulet and P. Baltes, pp. 485-507. New York: Academic Press.

_____. 1965. "A General Model for the Study of Developmental Problems." *Psychological Bulletin* 64:92-107.

Schaie, K. W., and G. Labouvie-Vief. 1974. "Generational Versus Ontogenetic Components of Change in Adult Cognitive Behavior: A Fourteen-Year Cross-Sequential Study." *Developmental Psychology* 10:305-320.

Schaie, K. W., and C. R. Strother. 1968. "The Effects of Time and Cohort Differences on the Interpretation of Age Changes in Cognitive Behavior." *Multivariate Behavioral Research* 3:259-294.

Simonton, D. K. 1977. "Creativity, Age, and Stress: A Biographical Time-Series Analysis of 10 Classical Composers." *Journal of Personality and Social Psychology* 35:791-804.

Starkweather, E. D. 1968. "Studies of the Creative Potential of Young Children." In *Creativity at Home and In School*, edited by B. G. Williams. Saint Paul, Minnesota: Macalester College.

Stern, F. H. 1967. "Creative Aging is Within the Reach of All." *Psychosomatics* 8:59-62.

Stevens-Long, J. 1979. *Adult Life: Development Processes*. Palo Alto, California: Mayfield.

Taylor, I. A. 1974. "Patterns of Creativity and Aging." In *Successful Aging: A Conference Report*, edited by E. Pfeiffer, pp. 113-117. Durham, North Carolina: Duke University Press.

Torrance, E. P. 1979. *The Search for Satori and Creativity*. Buffalo, New York: Creative Education Foundation.

_____. 1977. "Creativity and the Older Adult." *The Creative Child and Adult Quarterly* 2:136-144.

_____. 1966. *Torrance Tests of Creative Thinking*. Princeton, New Jersey: Personal Press.

_____. 1962. *Guiding Creative Talent*. Englewood Cliffs, New Jersey: Prentice-Hall.

Troll, L. 1982. *Continuation: Adult Development and Aging*. Monterey, California: Brooks-Cole.

Welford, A. T. 1958. *Aging and Human Skill*. Oxford: Oxford University Press.

Williamson, J., L. Evans, and A. Munley. 1980. *Aging and Society*. New York: Holt, Rinehart and Winston.

Woodworth, R. S. 1921. *Psychology: A Study of Mental Life*. New York: Henry Holt and Company.

Zuckerman, H. 1967. "Nobel Laureates in Science: Patterns of Productivity, Collaboration, and Authorship." *American Sociological Review* 32:391-403.

II

APPLIED THEATRE ARTS AND THE ELDERLY

Senior Actors

INTRODUCTION

In 1966, as part of my acting training, I was assigned to work with Vietnam War veterans who were just beginning to fill the hospitals and receive public attention. At the time, I questioned my acting coach's motivations regarding this assignment, but accepted her request, and found myself standing in the middle of a hospital room in the Washington, D.C., area presenting monologues that I had painstakingly prepared. I was unsure of what my audience's reaction would be and even more unprepared for my own reaction.

Some cried at the funny parts and laughed at the serious moments and some remained void of any reaction at all. Others traveled with me as I attempted to create various characters and situations. When I returned to school, I asked my coach about my performance and for her insights into the various responses I had received. Her reply: "Well, some are on painkillers, some have lost their minds, and some just won't stand for anything less than an honest moment of acting." I thought about that for a long time.

Ten years later I found myself facing a similar audience of elderly people in a nursing home. Some laughed, some cried, and some were void of any reaction. Others were completely involved in the story and responded by laughing and crying at the appropriate moments. I became intrigued by this special audience, who were segregated from the mainstream of society, yet demonstrated a need for either theatre art or some sort of art therapy.

While an instructor at Virginia Commonwealth University, I began to work with special audiences in theatre including the handicapped, the institutionalized, and the elderly. Two courses were implemented, "Theatre Arts for Older Americans" (an intergenerational course open to seniors and undergraduates) and "Applied Theatre Techniques," which explored the value of these special populations as theatre artists. Although the work was largely therapeutic at the time, the term "applied theatre" was developed in an effort to combine informal therapy with theatre arts talent, the focus being on the talent of the participant rather than on the therapy.

It was during this time that senior adult theatre groups were being recognized, regionally and nationally, for their artistic gifts and innovative techniques.

More recently, two publications documenting the formation and implementation of theatre techniques used with senior adults have provided us with invaluable information concerning the development and refinement of senior adult theatre groups. Thurman and Piggins's (1982) *Drama Activities With Older Adults* and Telander, Quinlan, and Verson's (1982) *Acting Up!: An Innovative Approach to Creative Drama for Older Adults* attest to the theatre artist's interest in working with older persons.

The growing public interest in the elderly has helped to strengthen the theatre artist's efforts to locate senior adults who are interested in either creative drama, oral history theatre, or participatory drama, and work with them in developing senior adult theatre groups.

What was once thought of as therapy for senior adults has now taken a turn, as elderly theatre artists perform for the public, schoolchildren, and share important lessons in history and promote an interest in reading through storybook theatre. They also share with the public the importance of values and coping with difficult economic times. They are the best teachers because they have lived through it!

As an acting teacher and director, I sometimes marvel at the talent of this generation in portraying a character or conveying an intimate moment onstage and one elderly person's response was, "Well, why not? What have I got to lose?"

In this particular study, seven sites were selected, five of which were in the northern Virginia area and two in Richmond, Virginia. The drama programs for the five northern Virginia sites are discussed here although all seven were involved in the design and measurement of the program.

The particular theatre techniques have been designed and redesigned over a ten-year period and will continue to take on different shapes and meanings as the years progress. For the elderly are a changing population, consequently, theatre artists and artists in general must be aware of their aesthetic needs and desires. The elderly population we, as theatre artists, work with today have not grown up with the media, as the elderly population forty years from now will have done.

However, there are some theatre and creative arts activities, exercises, and projects that are timeless, and it is hoped that the senior adult theatre programs, whether they be formal companies or informal groups, will continue to grow.

Applied theatre assumes the talents and gifts of the senior adult; and because it is inclusive of almost every major drama technique, one should be able to unveil, encourage, or develop some "gift" in every person, regardless of age or handicap.

REFERENCES

Telander, M., F. Quinlan, and K. Verson. 1982. *Acting Up!: An Innovative Approach to Creative Drama for Older Adults.* Chicago, Illinois: The Coach House Press.

Thurman, A., and C. Piggins. 1982. *Drama Activities With Older Adults: A Handbook for Leaders.* New York: The Haworth Press, Inc.

3

COLLECTIVE IMAGES OF AGING: THE PLAYWRIGHT'S INFLUENCE

Though difficult to measure, the impact of dramatic literature upon the masses has resulted in a collective image of acting. The power of the playwright's script, whether crafted for television, radio, or live theatre, continues to influence a public perspective with regard to aging. The serious playwright seeks to unveil some universal truth through either comedy, tragedy, melodrama, musical theatre, docudrama, or opera.

Since the times of ancient Greece, the audience's involvement in the play has been vital to the playwright's craft. The Greek's commitment to theatre is best described in Hatlen's *Orientation to the Theatre*:

> It will be recalled the theatre of Greece was a religious institution which every free male attended as a public and sacred duty at the two main festivals, in midwinter and early spring. The City of Dionysia which offered competition in tragedies, was a profoundly serious occasion. The audience did not come to be amused or titillated. They came to share in the great searching problems of mankind--problems which elevated the human spirit through suffering.

The Athenian audience was a remarkable one because of their great zest for living and thinking (p. 275).

The Greek audience was equally devoted to comedy, and Aristophanes provided them with ample opportunities to laugh at themselves and at political leaders of the time.

A careful examination of how senior adults have been portrayed over the ages in comedy and tragedy leaves us with impressions of the elderly as both fools and wisemen. The importance of such an examination lies in the elderly's reaction to dramatic productions and the general public's image of aging.

As more and more senior adults become involved in theatre programs, the demand for appropriate scripts increases. And although many senior adult theatre programs center on creative dramatics and improvisational theatre, others have progressed to formal, scripted productions.

At each of the five experimental project sites we discuss in this book, the drama leader gave an informal introductory lecture concerning the images of aging in dramatic literature. As a result, participants became more aware of media programming that dealt with aspects of aging or included elderly characters in the cast.

The following philosophy was presented, in an informal way, to group participants. The senior adults were first introduced to examples of images of aging in Greek theatre.

THE GREEK PLAYWRIGHT'S IMAGE OF AGING

When considering Greek playwrights, the drama leader selected Aristophanes' *Lysistrata* (411 B.C.) as an example of comedy and Euripides' *Medea* to exemplify tragedy. In his essay entitled, "The Essence of Tragedy," Maxwell Anderson (1938) gave recognition to the influence of Greek theatre:

> However unaware of it we may be, our theatre has followed the Greek patterns with no change in essence, from Aristophanes and Euripides to our own day. Our more ribald comedies are simply our approximation of the Bacchic rites of Old Comedy (p. 513).

If one examines the various characters in *Lysistrata*, the conclusion might be that they are one dimensional and stereotypical, thereby nonrepresentational of the women, men, or elderly of the times. However, upon closer examination, the viewer may see various examples of women, both young and old, and elderly men, both strong and weak.

> But, O manliest grandmothers, onward now!
> And you matronly nettles don't waver!
> but continue to bristle and rage, my dears, for you've still got the wind in your favor! (p. 69)

The implication that older women, even grandmothers, were needed for the antiwar effort exemplifies the playwright's perceptions concerning aging women, and, thus, either reflects or influences the audience's perception of aging. Aristophanes, then, presented both positive and negative images of aging.

The main theme of the play, however, concerns his antiwar philosophy and not the plight of the elderly; consequently, the audience was probably more concerned with the parallels between their real life experiences, "for at the time *Lysistrata* was produced, Athens had suffered major military defeats by Sparta" (Aristophanes, p. 51). But the fact that the old people are presented as vital characters needed in the support of both sides of the argument about the necessity of war attests to some importance Aristophanes gave to the aging process.

Euripides also gives a mixed review of the aging process. The nurse in Medea, for example, implores the old servant to tell her of plans that will affect the nurse's mistress. She approaches the aging Tutor with respect in saying, "No, no, by your wise old beard I beg you, don't hide anything from your fellow servant!" (Act I, scene i).

The Tutor provides the audience with yet another insight into the image of aging as he explains to the Nurse:

> Well, as I was passing the usual place where the old men sit playing draughts, I happened to overhear one of them saying that Creon, king of the land, intends to send these children, and their mother from Corinth, far away into exile. But whether it was the truth he was speaking, I do not know; I hope and pray it wasn't the truth. (p. 303)

In describing the old men of Corinth as sitting and playing checkers in the "usual place," one is given a very different view from the old men of *Lysistrata*, who must fight against the women of the town. Simone de Beauvoir states, "But in Euripides it is the pessimistic view of old age that prevails." (de Beauvoir, 1972).

Of the old men in *Lysistrata*, de Beauvoir states, "The old men adopt Creon's views and try to recapture the citadel. Their warmongering attitude makes them odious and what is more they cover themselves with ridicule: their impotent fumblings provoke

We see certain strength in the character of Lysistrata as she assumes the role of leader and organizes the women of the town and convinces them to abstain from all womanly duties and responsibilities until the men agree to end their war efforts. On the other hand, we are also presented with the opposite view in the following exchange between Lysistrata and Kalonike:

KALONIKE

Hello, Lysistrata. What are you so upset about? Don't scowl so, dear. You're less attractive when you knit your brows and glare.

LYSISTRATA

I know, Kalonike, but I am smoldering with indignation at the way we women act. Men think we are so gifted for all sorts of crime that we will stop at nothing.

KALONIKE

Well, we are, by Zeus!

LYSISTRATA

But when it comes to an appointment here with me to plot and plan for something really serious they lie in bed and do not come (Aristophanes, p. 55).

The elderly men are presented in various manners, perhaps the most demonstrative being "when the chorus of middle-aged women sing of a goddess putting out fires, an old man urinates noisily" (Aristophanes, p. 51). They are also depicted as having a sense of determination as they struggle to the Acropolis:

ONE OLD MAN

Lead on! O Drakes, step by step, although your shoulder's aching and under this green olive's great weight your back be breaking!

ANOTHER

Eh, life is long but always has more surprises for us!
Now who'd have thought we'd live to hear *this*, O Strymodorus? (p. 61)

One old man adamantly protests the actions of the women and cries:

They'll never have the laugh on me!
   Though I may not look it,
I rescued the Acropolis
   when the Spartans took it
about a hundred years ago. . . . (p. 61)

The chorus of women reminds the audience of the potential strength of the elderly females:

bitter mockery from the young women" (p. 157). It should be pointed out, however, that the women, at this point, mock all men who are not responsive to their cause to end the war. Furthermore, had the men, young or old, agreed with Lysistrata at the beginning of the play, Aristophanes would not have had a viable dramatic conflict and thus an avenue through which to express his personal political views.

Although Euripides and, fifty years later, Aristophanes wavered between pessimism and optimism concerning the aging process, Shakespeare carefully developed and refined his observations of life and the aging process.

SHAKESPEARE'S IMAGE OF AGING

It is important to understand that during the time of Elizabethan drama, 35 to 40 years of age was thought to be the declining stage of life. In reviewing Shakespeare's work, beginning with his earlier plays, which place an emphasis on the physical infirmities of old age, and culminating with *King Lear*, and a certain respect for old age, one senses a keen insight through the playwright's poetry.

Shakespeare's *Comedy of Errors*, performed at Gray's Inn on December 25, 1594, provides us with Aegeon's negative self-concept as he tries to convince one of his lost twin sons that he is, indeed, his father:

Though now this grained face of mine be hid
In sap-consuming winter's drizzled snow,
And all the conduits of my blood froze up,
Yet hath my night of life some memory,
My wasting lamps some fading glimmer left,
My dull deaf ears a little use to hear:
All these old witnesses--I cannot err--
Tell me thou art my son Antipholus (Act V, Scene i).

The Duke blames Aegeon's mistake in identity on the infirmities of old age in saying:

I tell thee, Syracusian, twenty years
Have I been patron to Antipholus,
During which time he ne'er saw Syracusa:
I see thy age and dangers make thee dote (Act V, Scene i).

The character of Lear, however, displays Shakespeare's more matured understanding of the aging process. "*King Lear*," states de Beauvoir, "is the only great work, apart from *Oedipus at Colonus*, in which the hero is an old man: here old age is not thought of as the limit of the human state but as its truth--it is the basis for an understanding of man and his earthly pilgrimage" (p. 245).

Draper (1946) suggests that an investigation of the traditional theories of the time that influenced Shakespeare's choices is helpful in understanding his perceptions:

> The Elizabethan, following the tradition of Aristotle, usually divided man's life into three major parts, and each of these into two or more subdivisions. Of these major parts, old age was, of course, the last (p. 123).

There was a danger, however, in following the teachings of Aristotle, for ultimately his image of aging led him to "remove the elderly from power; for he looked upon them as beings on the wane" (de Beauvoir, p. 167).

Elizabethans also had the opportunity to review scientific theories of aging and found that they differed very little from the unhappy conclusions made by Aristotle. Fourteen years after *The Comedy of Errors* was produced, Henry Cuffe published *Differences of the Ages of Mans Life* in 1607, and Draper, in his investigations of Cuffe's work says:

> Medical writers regularly agree with Cuffe that the latter years of life are astrologically unfortunate; and that the body is dominated by black bile, cold, dry melancholy humor. This was the humor of bodily decrepitude and mental instability, and it easily gave way to the childishness of dotage. This is the evolution so aptly pictured in *King Lear* (p. 123).

The production of *King Lear*, while seemingly representative of negative aspects of aging, also provided the audience with the depiction of growing old as a part of the process of evolution rather than as a separate entity. And in the character of Lear audiences found a pathetic and sympathetic character with whom they might identify, consequently learning a more profound lesson in aging than Shakespeare had presented in earlier plays. *King Lear*, then, became a personal challenge to the Elizabethan audience as they observed in the King deterioration brought about by the circumstances of life and the aging process.

Simone de Beauvoir gives us a clue to Shakespeare's motivation for developing such a character in saying, "Many people have asked what reasons Shakespeare can have had for writing *King Lear*, that is to say for incarnating humanity in an aged man. Perhaps he was so moved to do so by the tragic lot of the aged in English towns and countryside--the fate to which they had been reduced" (p. 147).

The public's reaction to such a display of sympathy towards the plight of the aging may have been one of confusion as de Beauvoir goes on to say, ". . . *King Lear* has, generally speaking, been the least well received and the least understood of all the great Shakespearean plays" (p. 248). Whether the audience received Lear as a romantic figure or merely an old lunatic, de Beauvoir says we do know that "the ancient world and middle ages looked upon madmen as having a certain sacred prophetic quality; and as old age frequently verged upon madness, it often combined in itself the two traditional and contradictory images of the venerable sage and the old lunatic" (p. 247).

In contrast to the Elizabethan audience, viewers of the Restoration drama presented an altogether different appreciation for the stage.

THE RESTORATION PLAYWRIGHT'S IMAGE OF AGING

Playwrights who wrote for the Restoration stage were challenged by a very different audience. Hatlen (1962) describes this audience as:

> . . . fashionable wits, fops, beaux, parasites, and women of easy virtue. So limited was the audience that only two theaters were active in London, despite the fact that the population had doubled since Elizabethan times. For twelve years one theater was sufficient to accommodate this narrow following (p. 277).

The Restoration drama, however, did contribute two interesting concepts that continue to influence and alter theatre production techniques today.

The first of these innovations was the presence of female actresses in the productions. In 1656, a Mrs. Coleman appeared in *The Siege of Rhodes*, followed by Mrs. Katherine Cory in 1660 in Thomas Killigrew's production of *Othello* with "A Prologue to introduce the first Woman to come to Act on the Stage in

Tragedy" (Duerr, 1962). The production of a serious drama, however, was an exception to the time. Restoration audiences preferred ribald and oftentimes crude comedies that concentrated on the physical sensuality of the young and the eccentricities of the old. But it was this very preference that provided the second innovation, which was an emphasis on intergenerational relationships.

One finds numerous examples in Restoration comedy in which an older aunt or uncle is responsible for the well-being of a young girl, who is, naturally, being sought by a young man.

In Sheridan's *The Rivals* (1774), Mrs. Malaprop is referred to by Fag as "an old tough aunt in the way" (p. 22). In Hershey's (1958) notes on the staging of *The Rivals*, he emphasizes the similarities in intergenerational relationships between Sheridan's play and Oliver Goldsmith's *She Stoops to Conquer*:

> . . . there is in each the elderly Aunt or guardian. In both plays she is ridiculously pretentious: In Goldsmith's comedy her pretention is to high fashion and elegant style; in Sheridan's to copiously erudite expression and amorous intrigue. . . . Both elderly ladies wield economic power to such a degree that their nieces must not marry without their consent (p. 22).

One might hope that Mrs. Malaprop in *The Rivals* would receive some respect, if for nothing else, for her financial stability. However, she is described in an intercepted letter, much to her horror, as ". . . the old weather-beaten she-dragon" (Act III, Scene iii). Despite this negative attitude toward Mrs. Malaprop, the audience cannot help but develop a certain affection for her and her misuse of language, thereafter referred to as *malapropism*, and exemplified in this paragraph:

> You are very good and very considerate, Captain. I am sure I have done everything in my power since I exploded the affair; long ago I laid my positive conjunctions on her, never to think on the fellow again (Act III, Scene iii).

The audience was delighted by Mrs. Malaprop's speech when she inserted *exploded* for *exposed*, and replaced *conjunctions* with *injunctions*. Duerr's description of the Restoration audience, however, gives them little credit beyond their ability to laugh:

> The almost sick feature of the English Restoration theater
> was its audience. Average citizens rarely attended plays;
> still dominated and dehydrated by Puritan doctrine, they
> stayed away from them as if from the plague. The
> audience therefore was largely an aristocratic one.
> Sponsored by the King and managed by the courtiers, the
> playhouse became play-pens for gallants, their mistresses,
> and fashionable fops; plays were no more than the talk of
> animated dolls; and the actors, limited to performing in
> two barely paying theaters from 1660 to 1682, could hold
> the attention of the cream of society only by flamboyant
> oratory, mannered wit, and plain ribaldry (p. 177).

The modern playwright has a difficult task in that his or her audience may resemble any or all of the previously mentioned types. The modern audience also may bring to the theatre the experience of having seen examples of classical Greek, Shakespearean, Restoration, and modern plays. Thus, the modern playwright and audience may share an eclectic image of aging.

THE MODERN PLAYWRIGHT'S IMAGES OF AGING

In the United States alone, theater goers may choose from contemporary comedy, musicals, serious drama, classical drama in revival at repertory theaters, plus telescript and film versions of any or all of these choices.

As recently as 1982, a Broadway revival of Robinson Jeffers's adaptation of *Medea* exposed audiences to the nurse, "an old slave woman," and the Tutor, "an old man." In comparing Euripides' passage about the "old men sitting in their usual place playing draughts," with Jeffers' adaptation, we find the contemporary version reads as follows, "I heard them saying when we walked beside the holy fountain Peirene/Where the old men sit in the sun on the stone benches. . . ." (Act I, p. 5).

Contemporary U.S. drama attests to an increased interest in the aging process. *On Golden Pond* was presented at the New Apollo Theatre in New York in 1979. The audience was introduced to the aging characters of Norman and Ethel Thayer as they spend what might be their last summer on Golden Pond. Norman, in approaching 80, becomes concerned with his death, and early in the play he and his wife argue about the numerical designation of old age. As Ethel attempts to describe a couple she has recently met while walking in the woods, Norman challenges her rationalizations:

ETHEL
Here, help me with this. They're a very nice middle-aged couple. Just like us.

NORMAN
If they're just like us, they're not middle-aged.

ETHEL
Of course they are.

NORMAN
Middle age means in the middle, Ethel. The middle of life. People don't live to be 150.

ETHEL
We're at the far edge of middle age, that's all.

NORMAN
We're not, you know. We're not middle-aged. You're old, and I'm ancient (Act I, Scene i).

The audience observes the developing relationship between Norman and his future step-grandson, Billy, who is quick to point out that he and Norman are 67 years and two weeks apart. As the drama unfolds, however, this intergenerational relationship blossoms, and Billy develops a deep affection for the old man:

BILLY
Oh, yeah, we have a lot of fun. We don't just fish, you know.

ETHEL
No?

BILLY
Nope. We make good use of the time. Norman makes me practice my French, and I make him tell me stories from the old days. You and Norman must have had a pretty nifty time way back then. I was surprised.

ETHEL
Uh-huh.

BILLY
It's good for his mind, you know, to dig back like that. Sometimes he calls me Chelsea.

ETHEL
Oh. Well, you probably remind him of her in some ways.

BILLY
Yeah. I always say, "Norman, you know I'm not Chelsea, I'm Billy." He's okay. I keep after him. (Act II, Scene i).

As early as 1954, television viewers were exposed to the problems of aging through Paddy Chayefsky's *The Mother*. In this realistic television drama audiences were asked to consider the problems of middle-aged children and their aging parents. The play opened with the following startling image:

Dissolve to: Close-up of an old woman, aged sixty-six, with a shock of gray-white hair, standing by a window in her apartment, looking out apparently deeply disturbed by the rain splashing against the pane (Act I, Scene i).

It is interesting to note that the scriptwriter refers to the age of 66 as being old. The description that follows is thoughtful, but far from gentle, as Chayefsky prepares the audience for the second visual image:

We pull back to see that the old woman is wearing an old kimono, under which there is evidence of an old white batiste night-gown. . . . The bed is still unmade and looks just slept in. The furniture is old and worn. On the chest of drawers there is a galaxy of photographs and portrait pictures, evidently of her various children and grandchildren. She stands looking out the window, troubled, disturbed (Act I, Scene i).

Part of this character's inner conflict stems from her need to be employed and her unfortunate experience of blacking out in a subway on her way to a job interview. Further complicating the Old Lady's dilemma is her 30-year-old daughter's concern and insistence that the mother live with her and her husband.

Despite her daughter's objections, the mother secures employment as a production line seamstress, but is soon dismissed for incompetence. In a moment of anguish, the Old Lady calls her daughter and son-in-law, who quickly arrive to take the mother to their house to live. Her explanation upon their arrival gives us some indication of her self-concept:

. . . Well, the truth is, I'm getting old, and there's no point in saying it isn't true. (*To her son-in-law as he sets the valise down beside her*) Thank you, dear. I always have so much trouble with the clasp. . . . Did you hear the stupid thing I did today? I sewed all the left-handed sleeves. That's a mark of a wandering mind, a sure sign of age (Act II, Scene i).

The television drama might have ended here, however, Chayefsky has yet another point to make about aging: after careful consideration, the mother offers an explanation for her change in plans and announces that she will return to her apartment to live, adding, "Work is the meaning of my life. It's all I know how to do" (Act III, Scene iv). The daughter, who once objected to her mother's insistence for independence, now expresses a more positive understanding and responds, "When I'm your age, Ma, I hope I'm like you." (Act III, Scene iv).

Both *On Golden Pond* and *The Mother* reached massive audiences with examples of realism characterized by some significant change or experience by the main characters. *On Golden Pond* presents changing and developing relationships between elderly parents and their daughter and between grandparent and grandchild. *The Mother* presents, in the end, a positive image of aging and intergenerational understanding.

The dramatic works cited here are a very small part of the volumes of the available dramatic literature that approach, investigate, or display aspects of aging.

Regional and community theatre groups have opened yet another avenue for playwriting through oral history drama. Both the Guthrie Theatre and Actor's Theatre of Louisville have developed successful senior adult theatre programs based on the oral histories of the participants. Plays that specifically address the problems of aging, the experiences of long life, and the magic of creative drama for senior adults began to develop at least 20 years ago. "One of the oldest senior theatre organizations is Portland, Oregon's Theatre of Feast, founded by Alberto Cereghino in the 1960's and claiming continuous operation since 1969" (Older Americans On Stage, 1978, p. v).

Through the innovative and conscientious efforts of theatre artists and playwrights, Senior Adult Theatre has reached a unique status and received recognition by such national organizations as the American Theatre Association. It is through the combined efforts of the elderly and theatre artists that audiences are being made aware of the problems of aging and the value of the life experiences of the elderly.

The combined and individual efforts of film and stage help shape the public's view of aging; thus, it is the responsibility of the playwright, producer, actors, and directors to present solid dramatic literature, whether classical or contemporary, which remains true to a fair interpretation of the elderly not as a group but as unique individuals.

Television and film have been extremely powerful in reaching the masses. Because the film director has the power to edit and focus camera shots, he or she also has the opportunity to guide and determine the viewing audience's perceptions of aging.

Balazss (1970) stresses the importance of this potential impact of any given film:

> The human face is not yet completely discovered--there are still many white patches on its map. One of the tasks of the film is to show, by means of "microphysiognomics," how much of what is in our faces is our own and how much of it is common property of our family, nation or class. It can show how the individual trait merges with the general. The "microphysiognomics" of the film can differentiate more subtly and accurately than the most exact of words and hence it acquires, beside the artistic significance, an important scientific function, supplying invaluable material to anthropology and psychology (p. 83).

Given these influences and a growing public awareness, senior adults now have the opportunity to present themselves as actors, playwrights, producers, and directors, and, more importantly, to share with the public newly formed images of aging.

It is because of a strong commitment to this philosophy of the impact of dramatic literature that the drama leader involved with the five experimental sites, before beginning any creative dramatic exercises, oral history interviews, or life-span assessments, asks the question, "How many of you watch television?" and waits with anticipation for a show of hands.

REFERENCES

Anderson, M. 1938. "The Essence of Tragedy." In *European Theories of Drama* by Barrett H. Clark, 1965. New York: Crown.

Aristophanes (411 B.C.). *Lysistrata*. In *17 Plays: Sophocles to Baraka*, edited by Bernard F. Dukore, 1976. New York: Thomas Y. Crowell.

Balazss, B. 1970. *Theory of the Film: Character and Growth of a New Art*. New York: Dover.

de Beauvoir, Simone. 1972. *The Coming of Age*. Translated by Andre Deutsch, Weidenfeld, and Nicholson and G. P. Putnam's Sons. New York: Warner Books.

Draper, J. 1946. "Shakespeare's Attitude Towards Old Age." *Journal of Gerontology* 2:118-126.

Duerr, E. 1962. *The Length and Depth of Acting*. New York: Holt, Rinehart and Winston.

Euripides (431 B.C.). *Medea* in *Question and Form in Literature* by James E. Miller, Jr., Roseann Duenas Gonzalez, and Nancy C. Millet, 1982. Glenview, Illinois: Scott, Foresman.

Hatlen, T. 1962. *Orientation to the Theatre.* New York: Meredith.

Hershey, G. 1958. "The Play" in *The Rivals*, edited by Vincent F. Hopper and Gerald B. Lahey, 1958. Woodbury, N.Y.: Barron's Educational Series.

Jeffers, R. 1946. *Medea*: Adapted from Euripides. New York: Nelson Doubleday.

"Older Americans On Stage." 1978. A Report to the Alliance for Arts Education of the American Theatre Association Senior Adult Theatre Project. Washington, D.C.

Shakespeare, W. 1594. *Comedy of Errors* in *The Complete Works of William Shakespeare*, 1936. Edited by William Aldis Wright. New York: Doubleday.

Sheridan, R. 1774. *The Rivals* in *The Rivals*, edited by Vincent F. Hopper and Gerald B. Lahey, 1958. Woodbury, New York: Barron's Educational Series.

Thompson, E. 1979. *On Golden Pond.* New York: Dodd, Mead.

4

CREATIVE DRAMATICS

Theatre began as a serious matter, ritualistic in energy and somber in thought. Viewers were lifted and transported through time and space to another world via the words of poets and the mesmerizing movement of actors. Egyptian theatre, with its rites and special meanings, gave man one of his earliest opportunities to explore the true inner nature of his thoughts and feelings. Greek theatre continued this personal involvement through its investigation of man's relationship to the gods. The words of the poets danced audience members into yet another dimension of human experience--the imagination.

Modern theatre carries on the tradition of imaginative involvement in a story through creative dramatics, which is ritualistic in origin and playful in discovery.

Void of a stage or a classical amphitheatre, actors and viewers become united by the space they inhabit. In traditional creative dramatics, there are no formal costumes, set design, orchestra, lights, make-up, or designated areas for the audience. The shared imagination within a space becomes the unifying component. All participants agree upon a respect for the creative choices of each other, thus alleviating preconditioned behavior that focuses upon success or failure. As one idea spurs another, the creative drama group will build worlds of creativity, role-playing, and problem solving. And it is because of this nonjudgmental environment that each participant is free to become as involved in the imagination of the drama as were the Egyptian and Greek audiences.

Until recently, the term creative dramatics was primarily associated with children. Now, creative dramatic experiences are far-reaching and may be found in any number of environments including role-playing for job training, advertising, and education. Consequently it is not only the child who is exposed to this theatre technique but adults as well. Adults who are either professionally or personally affected by creative dramatics may find the experience, according to the focus and delivery of the lesson, either joyful and rewarding or frustrating and disdainful. For example, let's examine a hypothetical case in which an employee is required to attend a training seminar and participate in role-playing activities.

Role-playing at this particular seminar requires the participant to either play himself in a hypothetical but close-to-real-life employment situation or to play the opposite--the recipient of his actions. Although one employee may find this an easy and perhaps even rewarding experience, another might shy away from such displays and fail unmercifully during the excercise. The success of the role-play depends upon the fail safe environment provided by and nurtured by the leader of the seminar. The success of the leader depends upon his or her understanding and respect for the imagination and his or her professional commitment to enable participants to become involved in an imaginative way.

The manner in which participants are involved in the creative dramatic experience dominates the stage and visibly illustrates the quality of the exercise. Although both employees may be involved in the same role-play, one may exhibit self-consciousness although the other seems secure in his role and focused on the task at hand. Successful involvement should closely resemble the aesthetic commitment of the Egyptian and Greek audiences. In order to successfully use creative dramatics techniques with child and adult participants, one must study and understand, as much as possible, the relationship of the classics to our modern theatre art and society. In gaining such an understanding, the study of the development of creative drama as a teaching, learning, and artistic tool helps us to understand the child's commitment to the imagination and thus the matured adult's involvement in such an endeavor.

PIONEERS OF CREATIVE DRAMA

In 1958, Geraldine Brain Siks, pioneer in the field of theatre education with children, described creative drama as:

> A group experience in which every child is guided to express himself as he works and plays with others for the joy of creating improvised drama. Improvised drama means children create drama extemporaneously. They create characters, action, and dialogue as they are guided by a leader to think, feel, and become involved in the issue at hand.

As Siks discusses the immediate importance of creative drama, Brian Way (1967) explores a larger influence on human development, beginning with the child and continuing on with the adult for a full development of personality. Way places an emphasis upon the importance of the development of personal imagination and says:

> Individuality is also concerned with originality and deeply personal aspirations; drama encourages originality and helps towards some fulfillment of personal aspiration, and this is important to the full development of personality because even among the best teachers there can develop a tendency to help pupils to fulfill only teachers' ambitions for them (p. 4).

According to Way, the drama experience allows individuals to explore and strengthen talents, both intellectually and spiritually, which, if practiced as a child, will continue to provide motivation throughout the life span. He stresses the importance of individual intuition in saying it is:

> ... the most important factor in the development of inner resourcefulness, and for much of life--certainly for that part called leisure--full enrichment depends upon this inner resourcefulness. If this is neglected, then substitutes become a growing necessity both as a means of simple escapism from a reality that cannot be faced and as a general titivation of facets of personality that unconsciously still demand some form of fulfillment (p. 5).

The value of creative drama in educational settings in the United States began through the efforts of many pioneers in the field of creative teaching, the most memorable being Winifred Ward. Her work in the public schools of Evanston, Illinois, during the 1920s and 1930s culminated in the publication of *Creative Dramatics for the Upper Grades and Junior High School* (1930).

Ward's work was followed by Geraldine Brain Siks. In her early book of 1958 entitled *Creative Dramatics: An Art for Children*, Siks identifies four general learning principles that she felt were strengthened through involvement in creative dramatics:

(1) It provides for self-realization in unified learning experiences; (2) it offers firsthand experiences in democratic behavior; (3) it provides for functional learning which is related to living; and (4) it contributes to learning which is comprehensive in scope (p. 41).

Ten years after Siks's ideas appeared, Nellie McCaslin became a force in the implementation of creative dramatics techniques in schools. Her philosophies supported the value of the original thought as a part of the formal educational process. In 1968 she published *Creative Dramatics in the Classroom* and brought to our attention the similarities in the learning objectives of both education and creative drama:

1. creativity and aesthetic development
2. the ability to think critically
3. social growth and the ability to work cooperatively with others
4. improved communication skills
5. the development of moral and spiritual values (p. 4).

McCaslin not only provided the field of education with a solid philosophical base for the development of the child but also suggested specific techniques for integrating drama with classroom lessons in history, music, science, and math.

Creative Dramatics and English Teaching, by Charles R. Duke, was introduced in 1973 and published by the National Council Teachers of English in 1974. Duke stressed the importance of the development of creative ability in students and traced the history of dramatic activity in the classroom to Edward Austin Sheldon, who, as superintendent of public schools in 1853, introduced methods for incorporating drama in the classrooms in Oswego, New York.

With the presence of creative drama in the classroom, one cannot help but surmise that its impact depends upon the experiments and experiences of these early pioneers in the field. Their commitment to the idea that creative drama is a necessity rather than a luxury was shared by other educators and artists who, over the one-hundred-and-some-odd-year period, developed our current support and philosophy concerning creative drama. In order to understand the elderly adult's involvement in such an experience, it becomes necessary to study first the child's involvement.

CHILDREN AND CREATIVE DRAMA

In a report to the First International Conference on Theatre and Youth, leaders in children's drama proclaimed:

There is in children a thirst for the marvelous and even more, a need of laughter and emotion. It must be fulfilled. The impressions of childhood always remain. It is necessary that they be worthwhile. Children who do not laugh become disillusioned men. Those whose hearts are not touched become men with hearts of stone. It is not to men that it is necessary to teach love, but to children (Chancerel, 1952, p. 57).

Most children have the intuitiveness to explore creative avenues but, depending upon their environmental stimuli, may lack various abilities needed for focusing free, creative thinking into successful modes of communication. Creative drama not only encourages a unique freedom in the thinking process, but also provides the participants with opportunities to channel the creative thoughts into tangible experiences, stories, poems, music, and ideas.

The child participant usually displays a willingness for complete involvement whereas the adult, in developing critical thinking, may tend to be judgmental and offer either a personal or professional critique. The child's ability to become involved in the task at hand must be nurtured from birth to five years. We usually refer to these earlier stages of artistic development as "dramatic play."

DRAMATIC PLAY WITH CHILDREN

Dramatic play begins when a baby is stimulated by a sound in the room, a smell, a color, and continues with the stimulus of toys. It grows with the child as he or she learns to play games and develop fantasy stories. Such games as "playing school," "cowboys and Indians," "space invaders," or "going to the stock market" offer evidence of the child's need for role models and creative choices.

Peter Slade has provided detailed studies of the development of the child and the relationship to creative exploration and choice. In describing the development of a baby's movement he says:

> Early creative movement is of the hands and feet, kicking, extension of fingers, and later, with hand in front, there appear swift sweeping sideways movements, quicker than we can do it. Later still, these become more controlled and develop into that imperious sweep which clears the table of a meal in one fine moment of time (1954, p. 20).

Slade goes on to state that ". . . careful observation helps us to link the movement, first of the whole arm (baby up till about two years), with the more localized movement, later, of the scribble when the child begins to draw. Thanks to the light shed upon this subject by the guardians of Child Art, the scribble is now seen as an important stage of development" (p. 21).

Accompanying the development of movement is the development of creativity, or intuition. When a baby first discovers games such as "peek-a-boo," or the dropping of an object from the high chair to be retrieved over and over again by the unsuspecting adult, the elements of both intellect and play are at work. It is the play, however, that has been given secondary importance in U.S. society.

In the development of a performing artist, one studies the aesthetic lifespan of the student and attempts to surmise the effects of dramatic play, role playing, and creative dramatics before beginning formal acting lessons. If a deficiency in the "dramatic play" years exists, the acting teacher must substitute appropriate exercises on an adult or young adult level that will enable the acting student to fill this void. If there exists a deficiency in role models in the participant's life, and thus, opportunities to role-play as a child, the instructor again must substitute appropriate techniques that will fill an important void.

When working with senior adults in creative dramatics projects, then, one begins with a lifespan aesthetic assessment, for an individual's history plays an important part in the present artistic experience.

LIFESPAN AESTHETIC ASSESSMENT

Many techniques have been developed in actor training that enable a performer to develop a character from any play. It is always interesting in a beginner's acting class to instruct actors to complete a characterization form based on their personal lives rather than on a character they are preparing to portray. Once the actors have studied their own lives they are more aware of personal experiences that they may choose to use as inner resources for their portrayal.

In working with the elderly, however, time-consuming forms present a problem, because some are frightened by paperwork, others cannot read, still others may be afflicted either with sight loss or with impairments of motor coordination skills necessary to write. The transference of this exercise to the senior adult, then, is made by asking the questions orally and using the form as a stimulus for group discussion. Depending upon the group, the session may be completed within one meeting, or it may continue for as long as the drama leader feels it is helpful to the functioning of the group and to the experience of individuals within the group. The following Character Lifespan form was used at all five project sites as a stimulus for discussion and as a tool for assessing individuals within each group:

CHARACTER LIFESPAN

A. ENVIRONMENTAL LOCATION
   1. Where were you born?
   2. What year were you born in?
   3. Who was president the year you were born?
   4. Were you born at home or in a hospital?

5. Describe your earliest memories of the house you lived in as a child.
6. Did you have brothers and sisters?
7. Do you remember any games you played as a child? Tell us about them.
8. Did you attend school? What memories of school do you have?

B. SOCIAL AND RELIGIOUS ENVIRONMENT
1. Did your parents have specific rules the children had to obey? What were they?
2. Did you attend church? Describe your religious upbringing.
3. Did you attend parties or functions as an adolescent? Can you tell us about them?
4. What memories do you have of courting?

C. AESTHETIC ENVIRONMENT
1. Did you like music as a child?
2. Do you remember any songs from your childhood or young adult life?
3. Did you ever draw pictures as a youth?
4. Did you like to read? Do you remember any books you especially enjoyed?
5. Did your mother, father, or grandparents ever tell you stories? Do you remember any of the stories?
6. Did you, as a child, ever have a favorite room in the house or a special place to go to? What made this room or place special to you?

Responses to these questions offer the creative drama leader information with which to assess the experiences and development of each person. The responses may also be recorded and used later in developing oral history scripts and booklets. Finally, the discussions that are spurred by such questions help individuals to form a group as they discover similar experiences and share past history.

The creative drama leader may add questions later that encourage detailed responses or cover other areas of experience, such as history and politics.

Accompanying this Character Lifespan assessment, a more simple and aesthetic exercise is the Group Poem. The Group Poem enables the drama leader and participants in the group to discover the feelings that are current and important to each member of the group. Group Poem also offers the participants a visual stimulus while providing an outlet for voicing opinions, ideas, and problems.

Each person is given a half sheet of brightly colored construction paper. On each sheet one of the following incomplete sentences may be written: (1) Today I feel _____. (2) Yesterday I felt _____. (3) Tomorrow I will feel _____. The participants are instructed to complete each sentence. All papers are then taped together to reveal a long chain of brightly colored paper that visually displays the feelings of each person. The Group Poem is then displayed in the room and each participant is asked to explain his or her choice of sentence completion. In so doing, the participants in the group and the creative dramatics leader become familiar with the current character assessment. It is during the discussion that the drama leader may also elect to use creative dramatics techniques by asking members of the group to act out their current feelings, to illustrate their emotions by using their bodies, or to make facial expressions that best convey an immediate thought.

Once an assessment has been made of past and current experiences, the creative dramatics leader is ready to begin a drama program that best suits the needs of the participants.

CREATIVE DRAMATICS WITH SENIOR ADULTS

Numerous texts have appeared that support creative drama as an effective teaching technique, but it was not until Gray's work (1974) and Isabel Burger's book *Creative Drama for Senior Adults* (1980) appeared that the theatre and health professions began to explore theatre with the elderly.

Based on her numerous years of experience working with both children and senior adults, Burger provides guidelines for implementing creative drama programs with senior adults. She begins by studying the similarities between the child and the senior adult involved in creative dramatics programs:

A. In both groups, the basic objective is to build a healthy self-concept in order to motivate enriching, creative human relationships.

B. In both groups, the best way to be comfortable with and love one's self is to get rid of self-pity, self-hate, self-pride.
C. In both groups, one of the most successful methods to use in eliminating self-centeredness is to become other characters, to think and feel as they do (p. 22).

Burger further suggests that the key to their differences lies in the years of experiences held by the older participant. Though both the child and the senior adult experience a need for satisfaction in life, and thus a positive self-concept, Burger states, "The rebuilding of this faith in one's self is more difficult with seniors because their hurts go deep and they have built protective walls very high" (p. 20).

With the aid of the Character Lifespan and Group Poem assessments, the drama leader is ready to design and apply creative dramatics techniques that best suit the needs of the participants. The beginning exercises help to promote an atmosphere of discovery, positive self-concept, peer support and approval, and enjoyment.

The following creative dramatics exercises were used at all five project sites in the preliminary stages of the growth of the theatre ensembles of seniors.

CREATIVE DRAMATICS--IMPLEMENTATION AT FIVE SITES

Step I--Preparation: Assessment of the Physical Space

One of the most important steps in the implementation of a creative dramatics project with seniors is preparation. Preparation may be divided into two categories, the first being Character Assessment, Past and Current, which we have already discussed. The second step in preparation involves an assessment of the physical space in which the seniors will work. Some important questions to ask in regards to the physical working space are:

1. Is the space accessible to the members of the drama group?
2. Are there tables, chairs, or any other furniture which might be used?
3. Are there possibilities for either visual or aural distractions?
4. Will it be necessary to rearrange the space to accommodate the group?
5. Is the space open to onlookers?

6. What are the dimensions of the space?
7. How is the space decorated?
8. What are the predominant colors in the space?

Site A was housed in an older section of an elementary school. A new addition to the original school had been built to house elementary schoolchildren. The older section was used as a nutrition and community center.

The nutrition center for the elderly consisted of three main rooms on the second floor of the building. One main room was used as a dining area and was designated as a place in which participants could socialize before the main meal was served. Bulletin boards lined the walls of the room and displayed information concerning programs for the elderly, nutritional guidelines, and social security benefits.

This main room was filled with tables approximately seven feet long and three feet wide. The seniors grouped themselves around the tables according to neighborhoods, friends, or church affiliations. They sat in the same groups at the same tables every day. To request a change in their routine by using the space for the drama group would have presented a threat to an already peaceful environment. Furthermore, not all of the participants in the nutrition program joined the drama group. Consequently, the drama program was held in a separate classroom and participants often presented their work to the remaining seniors in the main room.

The room made available to us was sunny and pleasant. Windows lined one side of the room, and on the other side a chalkboard proved helpful in planning and organizing our thoughts.

The room was divided into three working areas (see Figure 1). Area "A" was used for participatory theatre that involved physical movement and large groups. Area "B" was utilized during smaller projects and creative drama exercises that could be accomplished either by sitting or remaining in a smaller area. Area "C" was used for visual and audio arts activities.

Located in a more heavily populated area, Site B served approximately one hundred people a day as compared to the small group of 20 to 25 people at Site A. Because of the increased number of participants at Site B, more space was available. The dining area differed from that of Site A: it was not self-contained but was open and spread out.

The dining area was partitioned off from an exercise and game area by brightly decorated portable bulletin boards. A small room

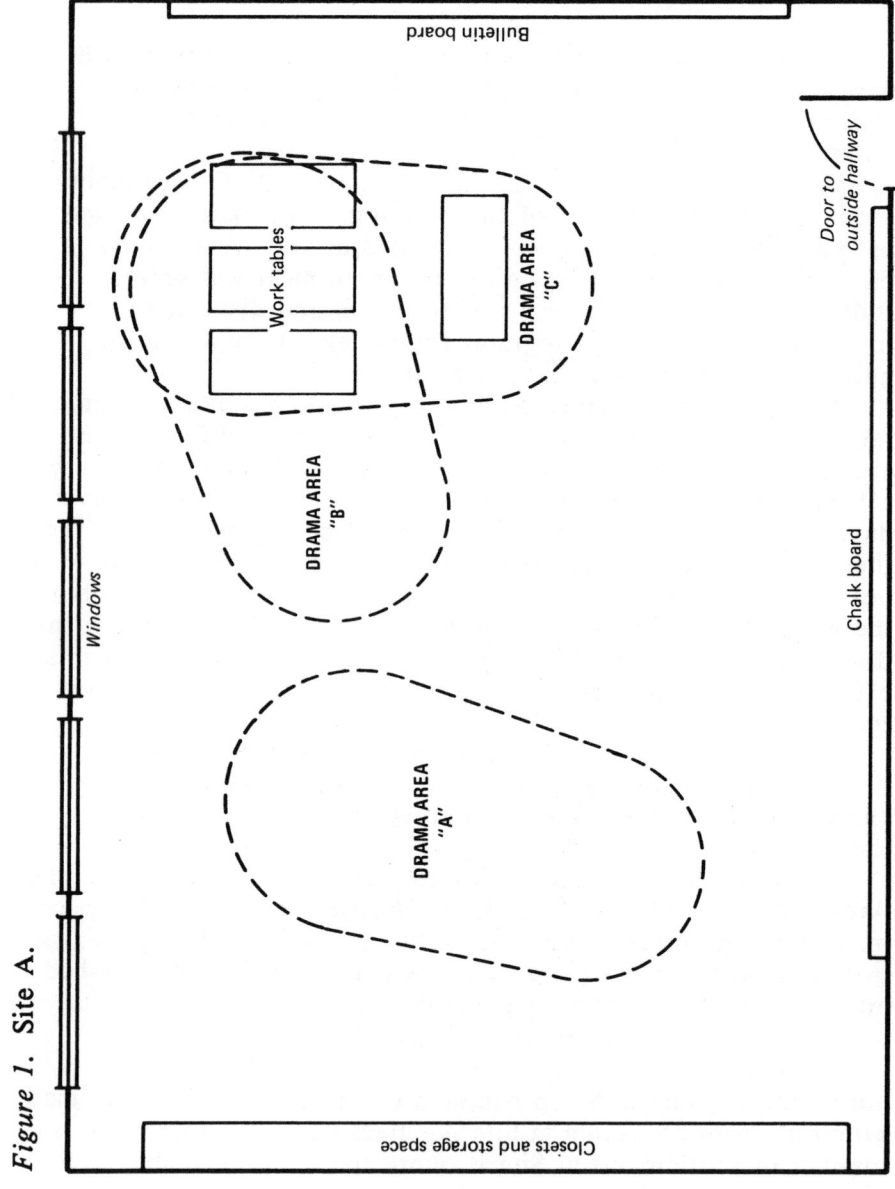

Figure 1. Site A.

off the main room was designated as the craft area. At the opposite end of the main hall was a medium-sized room, tastefully decorated with upholstered chairs and couches. This particular room offered the participants an area for concentration and was designated as the drama room.

Although preparation and exercises were practiced in this room (see Figure 2), the drama group also utilized parts of the main dining room for their performances and demonstrations, thus incorporating nonparticipants as passive members of the group.

A large kitchen located adjacent to the dining area provided an atmosphere reminiscent of an old-fashioned country kitchen. (This was an interesting change from Site A, where meals were delivered to the site.) The open counter space between the kitchen and the dining area provided seniors with a feeling of being at home because cooking was a constant activity at this site. The kitchen also provided the site with the necessary equipment to host international food days and other activities that involved the culinary expertise of the seniors.

Site B also functioned as a community center, thus, any number of activities were available to the public. The drama group had access to groups of children who attended afternoon and after-school programs at the Site.

Site C was very much like Site B in that it too was heavily populated, offered community programs, and contained a kitchenette. This site, however, proved more difficult to work in because there was no available separate space to work in. It did, however, offer a stage, which altered the implementation of the overall drama project. Participants here were more interested in using the formal stage and performance than were participants at other sites in which formal performance areas did not exist.

The drama group at Site C worked in two different areas. Area "A", though heavily traveled by people not involved in the drama group, proved to be an ideal space for creative dramatics exercises that did not require uninterrupted concentration but rather encouraged spontaneous involvement. Area "B" was used for demonstration and final performance (see Figure 3).

Site D differed from any of the other sites in that three separate rooms had specific functions within an elementary school. This site was divided into three large classrooms, one set up with tables for a dining area, another designated as the arts and crafts room, and a third as a general room for special activities and relaxation. It was in the third room that the drama group met and worked.

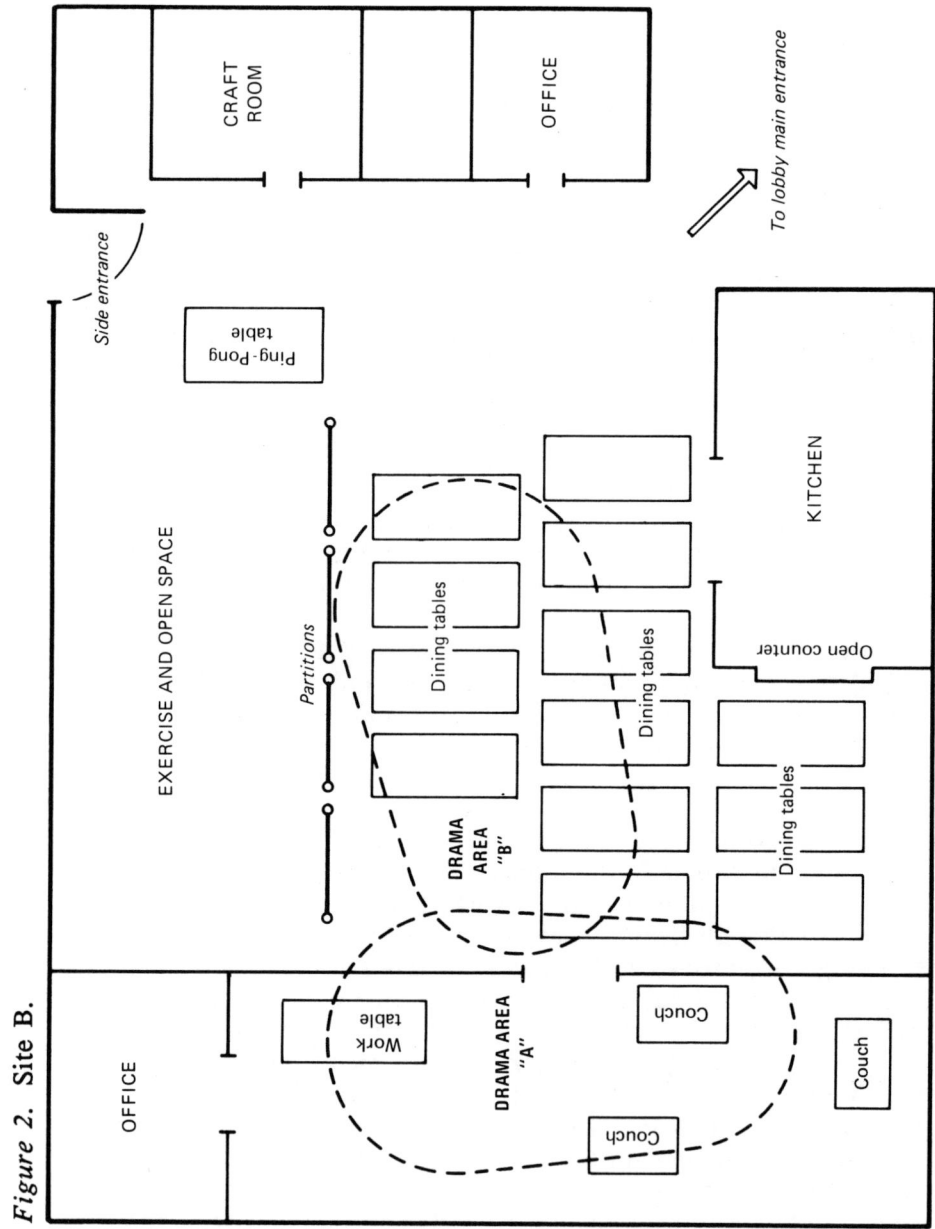

Figure 2. Site B.

Figure 3. Site C.

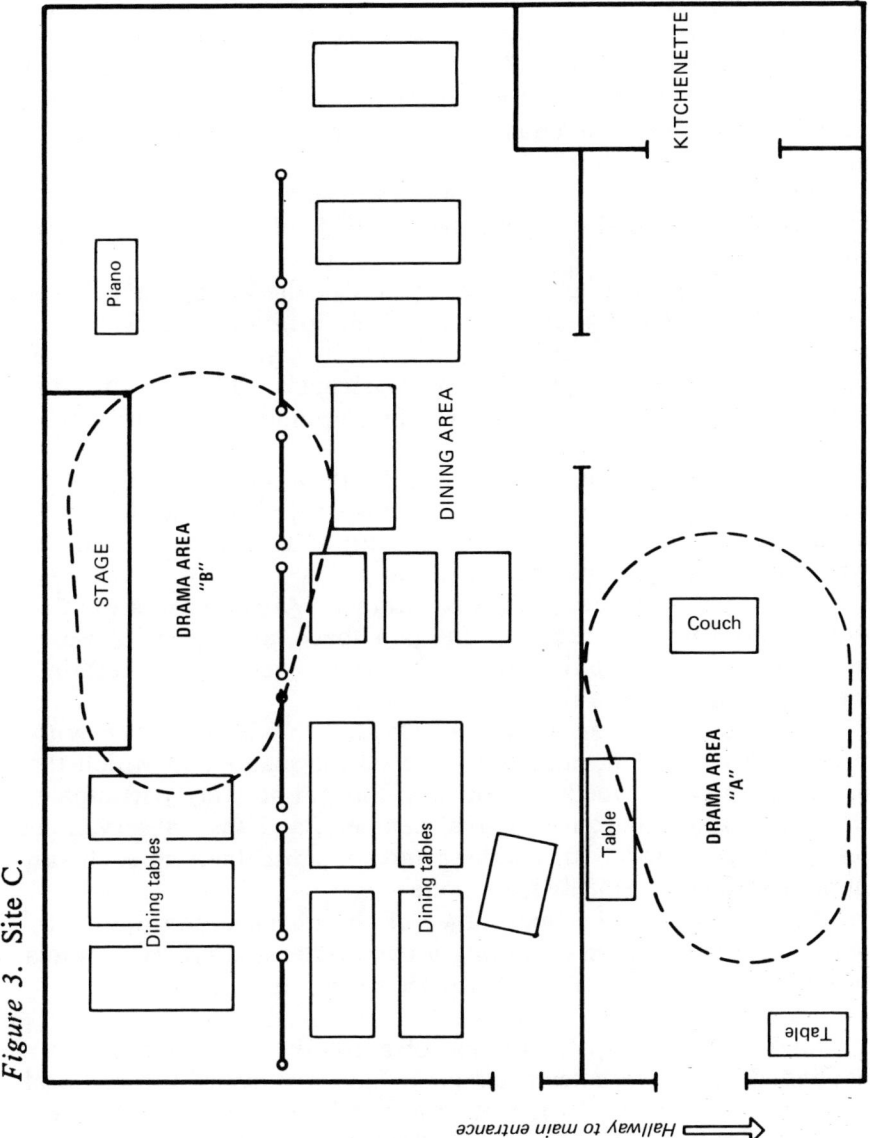

Three separate drama areas were established according to the needs of specific theatre projects. Tables were moved and chairs rearranged to accommodate the members of the drama group.

Area "A" was used for large participatory dramas, whereas areas "C" and "B" were used for exercises that required less space. Intergenerational theatre projects were held in a separate music room that was not a part of the nutrition site, but was one for the use of which we received permission. The music room contained raised platforms and adequate space to accommodate 20 senior adults and 16 children.

The regularly designated room for drama was crowded, but comfortable, especially after rearrangement of existing furniture (see Figure 4).

Site E, located in an elementary school, had two connected classrooms as its designated space. The location of these classrooms differed from the other sites in that they were located on the same halls as regular school classrooms. Thus senior adults were exposed daily to children walking up and down the halls, arriving and leaving school.

Dining, crafts, relaxation, and recreation were all offered within this space without any partitions or dividers. Consequently, the drama group had a constant audience in other seniors who had not joined the theatre group.

Two areas were designated for drama. Area "A" was used for drama activities that required an open space, and Area "B" was used for preparing audio-visual materials to accompany certain theatre projects (see Figure 5).

The presence of an audience provided the drama group with instant peer reaction, and, thus, altered the manner in which the drama group developed. Those who did not actively participate in the drama group became passive members, and they observed each session and reacted with laughter and thoughtfulness to each skit, improvisation, or oral history scene.

In all five sites the importance of the physical environment was considered before designing a comprehensive creative drama program. The availability of children for intergenerational programming was also taken into account.

Step II in the implementation of a creative dramatics program depended upon character assessments and a study of the physical environments, for without these the overall process would have been incomplete. Whereas Step I focused upon the physical environment, Step II focused on the aesthetic environment.

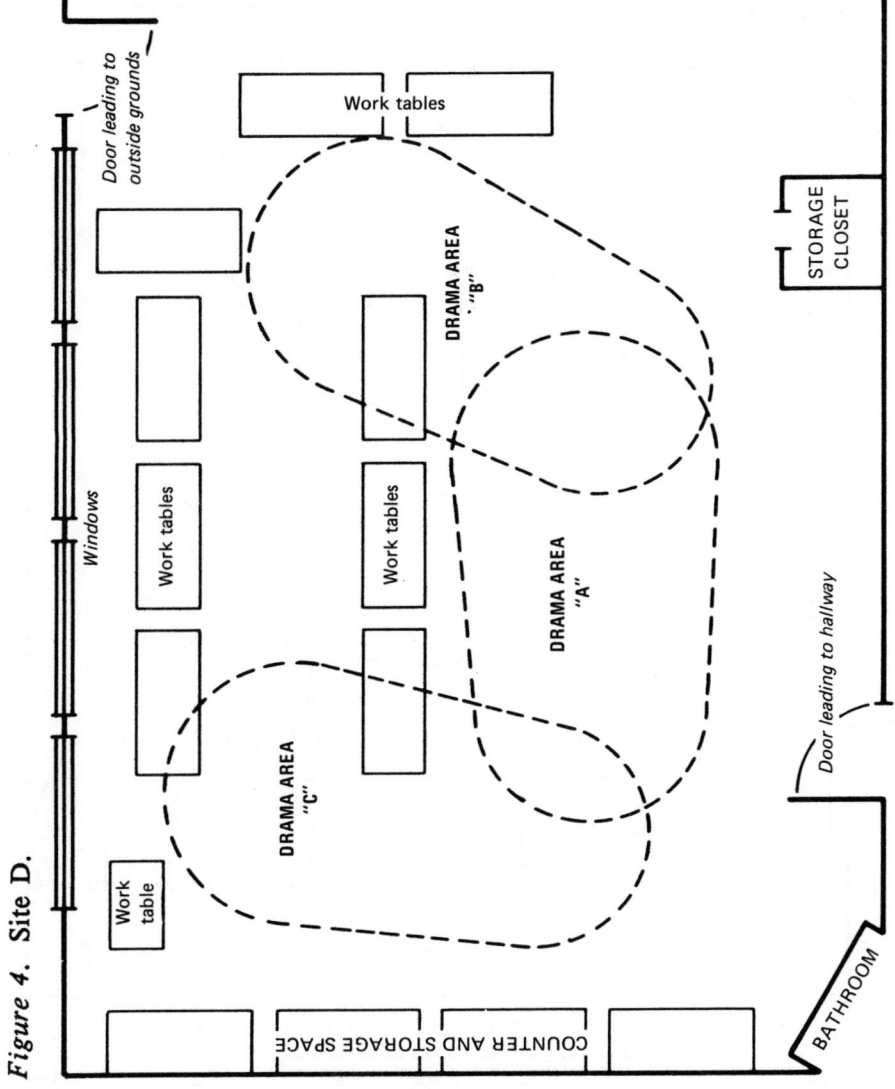

Figure 4. Site D.

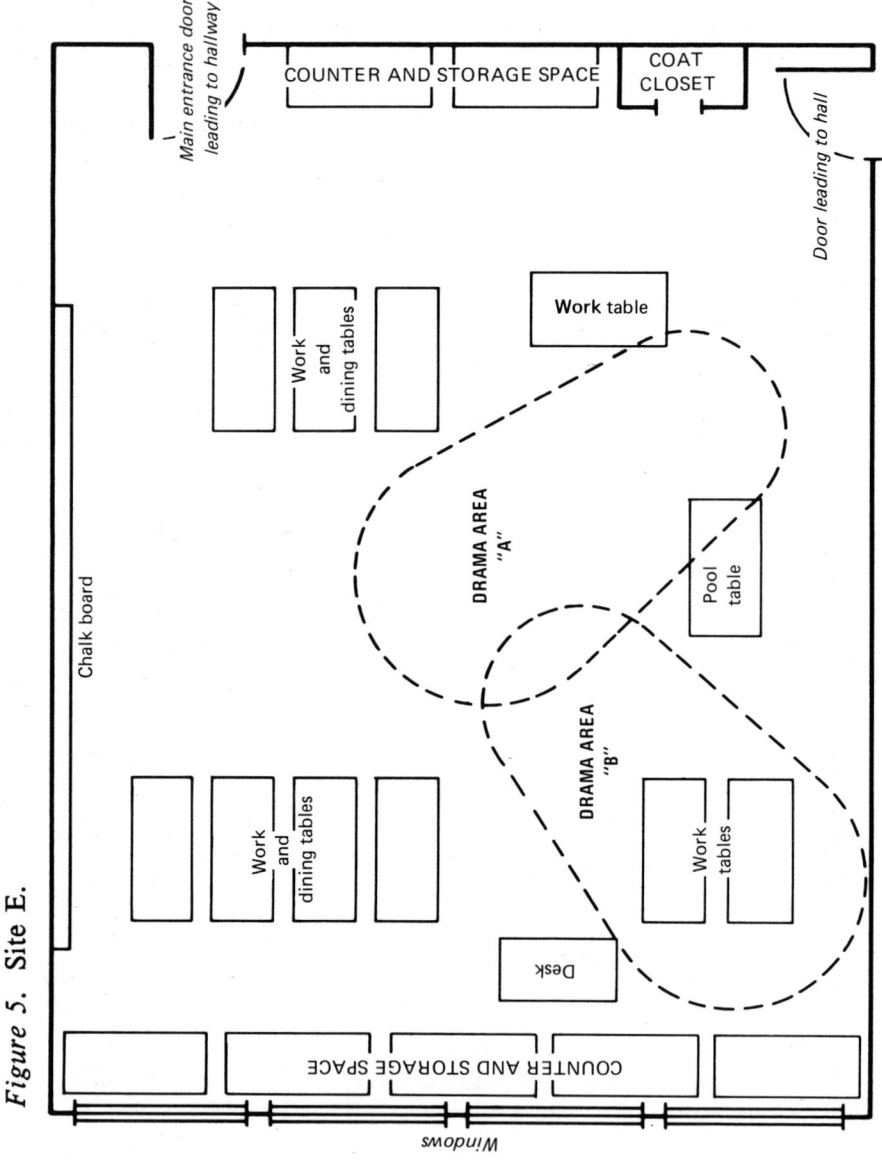

Figure 5. Site E.

Step II--Establishing an Aesthetic Environment

The availability of musical instruments, art supplies, and individual talents is of obvious importance to the creative dramatics program. But more importantly, it is the incorporation of these resources into the overall design that affects the quality of the experience. Recognizing individual gifts within the group helps to establish self-confidence and a certain excitement as seniors realize their abilities and feel able to continue to make contributions to the community.

If, for example, we work with an 80-year-old black woman whose profession was domestic helper, who sang gospel music from the time she could open her mouth, and remembers rich folk-tales told by her grandmother of swamp nights and sounds of the South, we should also recognize her potential gifts and contributions. Her life experiences in working for people, her love of music, and her wealth of stored folktales can make a tremendous contribution to the group and to the community.

This sense of experience is what makes creative drama with the elderly such a rewarding experience. If a senior adult is truly involved, as the child is or Greek audiences were, in the dramatic experience, he or she will bring to the moment not only exploration and discovery but the knowledge of living, as well. It is important, then, in establishing an aesthetic environment to recognize individual potential and to make each senior aware of his or her individual experiences and talents as a major factor in the success of the group.

Many senior adults have been more aware throughout their lifespans and can offer monumental insights. Others use the time during their retirement for retrospect and a sorting out of the truth. Still others have had little experience with observing life and it is during the creative dramatics experience that they begin to discover the eminent value of their lives.

Both the Group Poem and Character Lifespan can help to establish an aesthetic environment. Through the process of the Group Poem participants are able to see a tangible artistic product and explore their feelings through physical or vocal interpretations. The Character Lifespan provides participants with an opportunity to reenact past experiences and to view these as potential oral history presentations.

Once participants have realized their potential talents, the drama leader may choose to introduce them to available creative drama and theatre projects that they might explore as a group. The space, then, is gradually transformed into an aesthetic, working, and discovering environment. Ideas, stories, and personal information begin to fill the room, and senior adult creative dramatics begins its development within the group.

The following tables illustrate this aesthetic development, which took place at the five project sites.

TABLE 3. Implementation of Applied Theatre Programs at Site A: Establishing an Aesthetic Environment

Exercise	Observation	Evaluation
Character lifespan	Participants eager to share stories	Participants have very few activities at this site and are enthusiastic about discussion
		Many have limited education
Group poem	Writing presents threat to those who are illiterate	Group displayed need to express day-to-day feelings within a support group
	Participants enjoyed verbal exchange and the acting out of feelings	Talking book series may be difficult due to illiteracy

Individual Potential: (a) one accomplished musician/guitar; (b) three very expressive in relaying stories.

TABLE 4. Implementation of Applied Theatre Programs at Sites B and C: Establishing an Aesthetic Environment

Exercise	Observation	Evaluation
		SITE B
Character lifespan	Participants shy at first	One participant shared problem and might have gained benefit from acting out of story
	Participants begin to find similar experiences	Some participants intent more upon listening than talking
Group poem	Participants share laughter and are interested in each other's selections	Participants lean toward lighter topics and perhaps more interested in comedy

Individual Potential: (a) possible oral history script based on first date experience; (b) wheelchair-confined participant interested in dance; (c) possible applied theatre candidates--sociodrama and role-playing.

		SITE C
Character lifespan	Participants hesitant to share answers at first	Difficult for participants to share personal experiences due to lack of concentration; space inappropriate for group discussion
Group poem	Participants quick to fill in answers	May be more difficult to establish a group feeling because there is a lack of a "quiet space" in which to share ideas
	Participants less enthusiastic about explaining answers	

Individual Potential: (a) two participants accomplished dancers; (b) one participant with background in photography.

TABLE 5. Implementation of Applied Theatre Programs at Sites D and E: Establishing an Aesthetic Environment

Exercise	Observation	Evaluation
		SITE D
Character lifespan	Participants enjoy sharing tales of (1) driving a car, (2) dating experiences (3) changes in the times	Participants very outgoing and interested in developing scripts. Participants make suggestions for future projects. Participants may be more open to aesthetics due to ongoing visual art program
Group poem	Participants quick to respond. Some help others in deciding upon an answer	Participants display an openness to helping each other and working together. Feel group sense has already been established by site director

<u>Individual Potential</u>: (a) one retired greeting card illustrator; (b) all participants enthusiastic about acting out oral histories.

		SITE E
Character lifespan	Participants eager to share stories. Participants suggest topics. Participants use vocal and facial expression while relaying stories	Relaxed atmosphere of site promotes congeniality; participants display openness to sharing stories and ideas
Group poem	Participants select both positive and negative responses and are eager to share feelings	Participants function as a group due to site environment established by director

<u>Individual Potential</u>: (a) participants display vocal and facial expressions in telling stories.

After establishing an aesthetic environment, the drama leader is ready to implement specific theatre techniques into the program. Many of the same techniques were used at each of the sites, but there were also individualized exercises. Because creative drama lends itself to spontaneity, each site developed a unique energy as a group and theatre ensemble. In Chapter 5 we will discuss the specific theatre techniques used at each site and their impact upon the aesthetic environment.

REFERENCES

Burger, Isabel. 1980. *Creative Drama for Senior Adults.* Wilton, Connecticut: Morehouse-Barlow.
Chancerel, Leon. 1952. "Report of the First International Conference on Youth," at the United States National Commission for UNESCO. Unpublished.
Duke, R. 1974. *Creative Dramatics and English Teaching.* Urbana, Illinois: National Council Teachers of English.
Gray, P. 1974. *Dramatics for the Elderly: A Guide for Residential Care Settings and Senior Centers.* New York: Teachers College Press.
McCaslin, Nellie. 1974. *Creative Dramatics in the Classroom*, 2nd ed. New York: Longman.
Siks, G. 1958. *Creative Dramatics: An Art for Children.* New York: Harper and Brothers.
Slade, P. 1954. *Child Drama.* London: University of London Press.
Ward, Winifred. 1930. *Creative Dramatics for the Upper Grades and Junior High School.* New York: Appleton-Century.
Way, Brian. 1967. *Development Through Drama.* New York: Humanities Press.

5

THEATRE TECHNIQUES WITH THE ELDERLY

Theatre techniques used with the elderly are closely related to those used with actors in professional training. Depending upon the theory of acting, a student is provided with creative stimuli and is required to observe, interpret, or expand upon a given idea. Specific techniques may include mirror exercises, character assignments, movement exercises, scoring a script (Stanislavski, 1949), shared character relationships, and silent communication.

For the senior adult, many of these exercises may be too intricate for the purpose of the theatre group. However, most of the actor training exercises have their beginnings in creative dramatics. Thus, we are able to transpose actor training techniques to fit the needs of the elderly participant. Some specific theatre techniques used at the five project sites include: (1) mirror exercises (Spolin, 1976); (2) group poetry; (3) improvisations; (4) oral history theatre; (5) talking book series; (6) participatory historical theatre; (7) fill-in-the-blank participatory theatre; (8) scarf and chair dancing; and (9) original scriptwriting.

Professional actor training and theatre work with the elderly do share some of the same goals, such as:

o   provide opportunities to improve communication skills;
o   provide experiences of focused observation;
o   provide experiences in silent communication with a partner;

o   provide opportunities for increased skills in observing movement; and
o   provide opportunities for shared space through nonverbal communication.

MIRROR EXERCISES

The senior adult and the professional actor share the same objectives in their efforts to improve observational skills and interpretive talents while exercising creative choices. For senior adults this may mean observing someone else's interpretation of their movements, gestures, and facial expressions.

As the elderly become more isolated from the mainstream of life, communication with and response to others becomes less and less a major part of their lives. Consequently, an awareness of one's own physical appearance and response to stimuli around them become lost. The mirror exercises help to emphasize the importance of physical language and nonverbal communication.

Viola Spolin provides us with numerous mirror exercises in her book *Improvisations for the Theatre* (1976). Perhaps the most appropriate mirror exercise for use with a beginning senior adult theatre group is Mirror Exercise # 1:

Two players.
A faces B. A is the mirror, and B initiates all movement. A reflects all B's activities and facial expressions. While looking into the mirror, B takes a simple activity such as washing or dressing. After a time, reverse the roles with B playing the mirror and A initiating the movement (p. 60).

This exercise provided the participants with a general view of their own physical movements. Other mirror exercises used at the five project sites included the following:

Mirror Exercise--Specific Focus

Two players. A copies the movements of B. The drama leader designates a specific physical area on which to concentrate. This area may be the right hand, the left arm, feet only.

B is instructed to carry on a conversation with A and use natural gestures.

Follow-Up Discussions.

1. The players discuss the movements and change places. B copies the movements of A. The specific area may be the same or the point of focus may be changes.
2. A and B compare their movements and ask such questions as: (a) How do our movements differ? (b) Did the verbal messages coincide with the nonverbal gestures?

Mirror Exercise--Undesignated Focus

Two players. A copies the movements of B. A selects a specific area of focus but does not reveal choice.

Follow-Up Discussions.

1. B guesses what the area of focus was. A and B discuss the movement patterns and the verbal message. The players change places. B decides upon a point of focus and copies the movements of A.
2. A guesses what the area of focus was. A and B discuss the movement patterns in relation to the verbal message.

Mirror Exercise--Group Focus

Four players. A and B carry on a conversation. C copies A and D copies B. The players may choose a general focus or a designated focus.

Follow-Up Discussion.

Other members of the drama group contribute to the discussion by sharing their observations of the 4 players. Such questions as (1) Did the verbal message coincide with the nonverbal message? (2) Were the players true to their real life gestures? (3) Did the players concentrate on the designated areas? and (4) What did the exercise communicate? are helpful in making the technique a meaningful experience for all involved.

Mirror Exercise--Designated Emotion: Negative

Two players. A is instructed to carry on a conversation with B. A has been given a specific emotion such as "anger," "fear," "distress," or "confusion." B copies all the movements of A.

Follow-Up Discussions.

1. A and B discuss the movements of A in relation to the designated emotion. A and B switch places and B is given a designated emotion. A copies the movements of B.
2. A and B discuss how their movements and gestures differ.

Mirror Exercise--Designated Emotion: Positive

Two players. A is instructed to carry on a conversation with B. A has been given a specific emotion such as "joy," "excitement," "happiness," or "giddiness." B copies all the movements of A.

Follow-Up Discussions.

1. A and B discuss the similarities and differences between the movements and gestures for positive and negative emotions. A and B switch places and B is given a designated emotion. A copies the movements of B.
2. A and B discuss how their movements and gestures differ.

Mirror Exercise--Silent Partner

Two players. A is given either a positive or negative emotion and instructed to carry on a silent conversation. B copies the movements of A.

Follow-Up Discussions.

1. B is asked to identify the emotion A was portraying. B explains his choice. A and B change places. B is given either a positive or negative emotion and is instructed to carry on a silent conversation. A copies the movements of B.
2. A is asked to identify the emotion B was portraying. A explains his choice. A and B compare gestures and movements.

The value of various mirror exercises is in helping the senior adult to become aware of physical communication with others. In observing another person's movement and communication skills, one becomes temporarily removed from making judgments and concentrates instead on the physical language. For the senior adults, this could mean a broadening of experiences as their personal philosophies change from evaluation and criticism to observation and response.

Verbal communication is as important as nonverbal communication. For the elderly, sharing real feelings with others is of vital importance to their continued existence. Other age groups, still involved in the mainstream of society, have friends, family, business associates, or some sort of human support system to which they may convey their feelings. The elderly, however, because of their forced isolation, often have a difficult time in finding this "human sounding board." Communication skills take practice, and if one is isolated from situations involving daily communication skills, they are likely to become lost or less effective. Lack of communication skills, then, may not be due to old age, but rather to the lack of opportunities to use these skills.

The Group Poem discussed in Chapter 4 offers the senior adult the opportunity to voice opinions and feelings without the fear of punishment. The following exercises were based on the Group Poem technique and used at all five project sites:

Group Poem--Free Verse

The leader distributes construction paper to all participants with different incomplete sentences such as:

My favorite person is _____.
A friend is _____.
My best friend was _____.
I feel happy when _____.
I feel lonely when _____.

o Instruct each player to complete the sentence.
o Collect the papers and tape them together.
o Display the group poem somewhere in the room.
o Have each participant explain his or her choice.

Group Poem--Seasonal

The instructions are the same as for Group Poem-Free Verse. The incomplete sentences might read as follows:

Christmas is _____.
Christmas used to be _____.
Thanksgiving is _____.
Thanksgiving used to be _____.

o A follow-up discussion might include how the times have changed in general and personal changes.

Group Poem--Feelings: Statues

The instructions are the same as for Group Poem-Free Verse. The incomplete sentences might read as follows:

Today I feel _____.
Yesterday I felt _____.
Tomorrow I will feel _____.

o Participants arrange other participants in still-life poses that convey the messages in the poem.
o The still-life pose may be brought to life and an improvisational scene enacted.
o Participants are asked to assume a facial expression that conveys each of the feelings.

Through group poetry and the possible acting out of emotions, participants are given the opportunity to voice and explore their feelings of joy, anger, confusion, boredom, loneliness, and frustration and at the same time receive feedback from their peers. The poetry itself becomes secondary as participants bring each individual line to life through improvisation, facial expression, or group discussion. This is the advantage of free verse. As Judson Jerome points out in *The Poet and the Poem* (1974):

> Free verse merely points up something that is true about all poetry, but inescapable in this form. Every line of poetry should be interesting in itself--for the *way* it speaks as well as for *what* it says (p. 100).

For the senior adult, every line is important because of its personal connection with the author. In acting out the sentence completions, participants test their choices of words and explore their feelings behind the words. We usually refer to this "acting-out" as improvisational theatre.

IMPROVISATIONAL THEATRE TECHNIQUE

The focus of this Renaissance theatre technique is best described in *Invitation to the Theatre* (Kernodle and Kernodle, 1978):

> The most popular acting companies of the Renaissance had no playwright; they were the Italian commedia dell' arte troupes, who in the sixteenth century and for two hundred years afterward entertained Europe both at cultivated courts and at noisy street corners. Each performer was a star, perfecting one role in a lifetime of practice. Yet the troupe took great pride in the way they played together. They made up the words as they went along, following an outline tacked up behind the scenes by the manager to indicate what episode was to come next (p. 293).

In professional actor training, improvisational work benefits the student artist by strengthening skills needed for concentration, focus, imagination, and awareness. For the senior adult, improvisational theatre affords the opportunity to develop strengths in communication, problem-solving, concentration, and creative choices.

A plot outline replaces any formal script and seniors are given the following information with which to build a scene, create character relationships, and invent dialogue:

IMPROVISATIONAL THEATRE

Plot Outline

Who: Designates characters in the scene
What: Designates the conflict of the scene
Where: Designates the location of the scene

It is usually best to begin with two characters, thus avoiding the confusion of too many people on stage at one time. This also enables the seniors to concentrate on one other character at a time rather than numerous characters. As senior become more advanced and experienced, drama leaders may choose to add more characters to the improvisation. The following improvisational techniques were used at all five sites:

Improvisation--Who, What, Where: "Stuck In"

Players: 2.
o   Remind participants that scene should have a beginning, middle, and end
o   Remind participants that they should concentrate on listening to the other character.
o   Participants draw a card from a hat that has any of the following situations:

Who: Two characters (either men or women or combination; allow participants to decide upon their relationship--*i.e.*, two friends, brother and sister)
What: *Stuck in an elevator*
Where: In a department store

Who: Two characters (One of the characters may be on the outside of the closet, while the other is stuck inside.)
What: *Stuck in a closet*
Where: At home

Who: Two characters (One of the characters may be stuck while the other plays the part of the store manager or a passerby.)
What: *Stuck in a doorway*
Where: In a drugstore

Who: Two characters
What: *Stuck in a bathroom*
Where: In a department store

Participants at all five sites gave their own personal examples of being stuck or trapped somewhere. For some wheelchair-bound seniors, these situations were similar to their own personal conflicts. Thus, a follow-up discussion was helpful and allowed participants to not only critique each scene but to voice personal frustrations. A second step in the Who, What, Where Improvisation, then, is to encourage seniors to use their personal experiences as a basis for an improvisational scene.

Who, What, Where--Personal Experience

- o Ask each participant to think of a personal instance in which they have experienced frustration and felt "stuck."
- o The situation may be based upon an emotional "stuck" rather than a physical "stuck" (*i.e.*, one participant had been forced to move in with her daughter and son-in-law. She felt "stuck" because financially she had no other choice).
- o Ask participants in the scene to carry the improvisation to the solution.
- o Ask other members of the group who are observing the improvisation to suggest possible solutions.
- o Ask the improvisational scene actors to incorporate one or two of the suggested solutions into the scene.

Follow-Up Discussion.

The drama leader may discuss the parallels between real-life conflicts and conflicts in drama. A discussion and review of how characters react to conflict in specific dramatic literature might be used to reinforce the lesson. For example, in Paddy Chayefsky's play *The Mother* (1954), the aging mother does not want to give up her independence. Parallels between the character's experience in the play and the real-life drama of the senior adult may be pointed out and discussed.

Who, What, Where--Character Focus

- o Ask participants to invent Who, What, Where situations.
- o Ask actors in the scenes to concentrate on the character rather than the conflict.
- o Ask actors to concentrate on physical movement, energy, and emotional response.

Follow-Up Discussion.

The drama leader should focus on encouraging the group to identify character traits and reactions. In so doing, participants may become more aware of their own response to an emergency or conflict and lessen their feelings of frustration while strengthening their understanding.

Up to this point, seniors have experienced exercises that enable them to be more aware of their physical and verbal modes of communication. They have become involved in observation of others and their relationship to the members of the group. They are now ready to progress to semiformal scripts, talking book series, historical drama, and participatory drama.

Again, the theatre techniques resemble those used in formal actor training. Seniors are now ready to use their inner resources to portray characters. Uta Hagen (1973), whose influence as an actress and teacher has played an important part in the development of actor training, describes the relationship between actor and real-life characters as:

> Once we are on the track of self-discovery, and we now try to apply this knowledge to an identification with the character in the play, we must make this transference, this finding of the character within ourselves, through a continuing and overlapping series of substitutions from our own experiences and remembrances, through the use of imaginative extension of realities, and put them in the place of fiction in the play (p. 34).

In professional actor training, performance artists are asked to develop their ability for sensory recall and use this stored information as a basis for their characterization. "Every stage of the search for the part needs endless substitutions from life experience (this includes reading, trips to museums, art galleries, etc.)" states Hagen (p. 36).

The senior adult participants, then, are asked to use their personal experiences as a basis for characterizations. The utilization of the self may be accomplished in two ways. The first method entails the senior's ability to recall moments of anger, cheer, frustration, confusion, and fright (to list a few emotions) and substitute these, where appropriate, to a character's response in a story. For example, if the seniors are acting out a children's story for a child audience and the story calls for an angry grandmother, the actor must recall moments of anger and use these experiences as a part of the characterization.

The drama leader may ask such questions as: (1) How does your body react when you are angry? (2) Recall a specific time when you were angry, (3) How did your anger affect your voice? (4) How did it affect your body language? (5) How did it affect your facial expression? and (5) How did your anger affect your response or relationship to others involved? After discussing the answers to these questions, the senior adult is ready to portray the angry grandmother, substituting his or her own body language, facial expression, and inner emotion.

The second method for utilization of the self in drama is through oral history theatre.

ORAL HISTORY THEATRE

Oral History Theatre may be produced in a very elaborate manner or on a professional level, as exemplified by the Actors Theatre of Louisville and the Guthrie Theatre. During the 1978-79 season, the Guthrie Theatre produced "Flashbacks--A Scrapbook of Personal Portraits" as a part of their Outreach Programming Office's special projects. This oral history project was described in the following manner:

> After compiling oral histories of many area senior citizens, the stories, memories, and resulting personal philosophies of seven of them were adapted into a 45 minute script. Experiences ranged from a close call with John Dillinger to the decision by a New York actress to give up her career for marriage, to a humorous tale about a woman who, at age 40, made a drastic change to make her appearance more attractive and was finally able to "talk back" to her husband. The stories contained in the final script are from actual experiences, concerned with "ordinary" people who led "ordinary" lives and are performed by the individuals to whom they happened (Guthrie Theatre, p. 1).

The advantages of Oral History Theatre begin with the aspect that it may be produced anywhere with either a great amount of technical assistance such as lights, sets, rear projections of photographs of the seniors as youngsters, costumes, and any other elaborate additions, or it may be just as successfully performed without the support of any of these things. Everyone, regardless of economic or social background, has memories to share. Senior adults, in sharing their personal stories, exhibit a pride and purpose in their life experiences through Oral History Theatre. The following techniques were incorporated into the drama programs at all five sites as a part of the development of Oral History Theatre.

ORAL HISTORY THEATRE TECHNIQUES

Senior adults must have some sort of stimulus to aide in the recollection of either significant historical events or personal experiences. Consequently, the drama leader with the help of the participants may suggest various topics for discussion. The following topics were used as stimulus at the five project sites:

CHANGES IN TRANSPORTATION
Horses and Buggies
o How large was the buggy?
o What did the buggy look like?
o Did you have a favorite horse?

Streetcar Rides
o How much did the streetcar cost?
o Do you remember your first ride on a streetcar?
o Where did you go on the streetcar?

Car Rides
o What car was the first you ever saw?
o When was the first time you ever drove a car?
o What did you have to do in order to start your first car?
o What did the car look like?
o Who taught you how to drive?
o Did you ever have an accident?
o How fast did the car go?
o Who was the first person in town to own a car?

CHANGES IN EDUCATION
o Where did you go to school?
o What did the building look like?
o What do you remember about your teacher?
o What did you study in school?
o How did the school you attended differ from the schools students attend now?
o How are the students different?

CHANGES IN FASHION
o How is the dress different today?
o Did you make your own clothes?
o Did you dress differently when your parents decided you were an adult?
o Describe the different clothes you wore.
o Did you have a favorite outfit?
o Identify from photographs and drawings fashions you wore or are familiar with.
o Sketch various fashions from your past.

CHANGES IN COURTSHIP AND MARRIAGE

o   What do you remember about your first date?
o   Where did you go?
o   What time did you have to be home?
o   What were some of the rules your parents stressed for dating?
o   How did you meet your spouse?
o   When did you decide to marry?
o   How was the courting custom different from dating practices of today?
o   How old were you when you got married?
o   How has marriage changed?

CHANGES IN POLITICS

o   Who is the first president you remember?
o   What do you remember about him?
o   What do you remember about the economy?
o   Identify from photographs and pictures presidents you remember and what you remember about them.

CHANGES IN COOKING

o   What was your favorite dish as a child?
o   What made it so good?
o   When did you learn to cook?
o   How does the cooking your mother practiced differ from the cooking of today?

The most effective way of introducing these topics at the project sites was through a game entitled "Oral History." The drama leader devised seven major category cards that had written on them: (1) Transportation; (2) Education; (3) Fashion; (4) Courtship and Marriage; (5) Politics; and (6) Cooking. Senior adults worked in pairs or individually, according to the number of participants at each site, and selected from a hat a major category card. Each participant (or team) then announced to the group the topic they had chosen. On a series of smaller cards were written the individual questions. Participants drew smaller cards, one at a time, and answered the question on the card.

As a visual stimulus, the drama leader had collected photographs, slides, and pictures from books and magazines that depicted elements of the major categories from 1900 to 1950. These visual aids were used at different times during the game. Sometimes visual aids were shown before participants selected a question card, and at other times they were used during discussions.

The discussion sessions that followed revealed unique individual recollections of historical events and personal experiences. After a time, each group selected certain personal accounts that they felt would lend themselves to improvisational scenework and eventually Oral History Theatre scripts.

As an outgrowth of the game and discussion, the following scenarios were developed and eventually presented to audiences:

SITE A

"Washington--This Must Be Heaven"

Personal experience: Riding from South Carolina to Washington, D.C.

Who: Storyteller, uncle, brother, and sister
What: Uncle taking children to Washington to be cared for by relative
Where: In the car

Significant dialogue: "I thought I was comin' into heaven as we passed over the bridge into Washington. I had never seen such things. Bein' dead asleep in the back of the car and then wakin' up and seein' Washington. I tell you I thought I'd died and gone to heaven."

SITE B

"Never Trust a Male Driver!"

Personal experience: First date with a fella' in a car
Who: Storyteller and date
What: Out on a date/boy not familiar with driving a car/puts his arm around girl and loses control
Where: Interior of car

Significant dialogue: "I just told him, never mind! I'd walk the rest of the way. Least I'd get there anyway! Men drivers!"

SITE C

"My Fling With a Trapeze Artist"

Personal experience: Storyteller met trapeze artist at party and elected to go away with him.

Who: Storyteller, people at party, boss, trapeze artist

What: Party is given in honor of storyteller/trapeze artist crashes party and impresses guest of honor with his ability to dance/storyteller leaves party with trapeze artist
Where: An office building in New York City
Significant dialogue: "I didn't know he hadn't even been invited to the party. I thought he was supposed to be there. Besides I had never known a trapeze artist, so I just went with him and asked questions later."

SITE D

"Tales of Stormy Nights"

At this site, participants had many tales of terror and combined their stories to show short vignettes of experiences. The following short thoughts were transposed into Who, What, Where plot outlines and acted out for children.

"It used to be that when there was a bad storm, you'd gather all the children in one room."

"I remember one night when there was a bad storm and I went and hid behind the couch. After it was over, my mother couldn't find me for the longest time.
When she finally did find me she asked my why I hadn't come out. Well, I told her that I was so scared when the storm came that I wiggled my way into a place and I couldn't get out. I was stuck!"

"I was at my sister's house when lightning came in through the window, blackened her silverwear, and went out the back door! We just sat there and didn't move . . . for hours!"

"It happened to me about a year ago. I had gone to the store during a storm and when I got home, my porch had a big hole in it!"

"Lightning went through my sister's house and took the roof right off and it never even touched the children in the upstairs bed! But they didn't move for a *long* time. Not even a peep!"

SITE E

"A Secret Kiss!"

Personal experience: Storyteller had promised a tryst with a young man later on in the evening
   Who: Storyteller as a young girl, mother, boy
   What: Girl is to meet boy down the street
   Where: In the house
Significant dialogue: "I would've walked ten miles through twenty feet of snow for that kiss!"

"A Secret Kiss" involved further work in improvisational acting as the group studied the circumstances surrounding the story:

> It is a winter night and the snow is falling. The storyteller continues to ask her mother if there is anything she needs at the store. The mother continually answers that there is nothing she needs. The mother begins cooking dinner. The snow is now falling more heavily. The storyteller is becoming more and more anxious with the passing of time. Finally, the mother says she needs butter. The storyteller runs out the door without a coat and forgetting to get money from her mother. The mother calls her back. The storyteller hurriedly takes the money and throws on a coat. She runs out the door. As soon as she is around the corner, she throws her arms around the boy and kisses him.

The basic information had been provided by the storyteller, but the drama leader felt that further characterization and motivation could be established. The question was asked of the storyteller, "Do you think your mother was watching you from the window?" The storyteller thought for a moment, smiled and said, "Probably." The following considerations were then given to the actors as a part of their character development:

1. It is winter, it is cold outside, and the mother is anxious to have a hot meal ready for her husband when he returns home from work.
2. The mother notices that her daughter is showing signs of restlessness.

3. The mother is curious about her daughter's behavior, but not anxious, and besides, she is preoccupied with preparing a good meal.
4. The mother discovers she is out of butter and there is just enough time for her daughter to go to the store.
5. The mother is surprised at the display of enthusiasm shown by the daughter when asked to run an errand.
6. The mother finds the daughter's excitement and forgetfulness interesting and looks out the window as the young girl runs down the street.
7. The mother smiles and remembers the time is drawing near for the arrival of her husband. A second thoughtful smile covers her face.

The senior adult portraying the mother in this scene was asked to use sensory recall, as discussed earlier in the chapter, while watching her daughter run down the street. The drama leader asked such questions as, "Do you remember a time when you looked forward to seeing someone you cared about?" and "Do you remember cooking a hot, delicious meal on a cold winter night for your family?"

Although the Oral History Theatre techniques and stories differed from site to site, one common element that continued to surface was the senior adults' deep commitment to their own personal story and the scenes of their peers as well. Several sites worked to make their oral history scenarios polished performances that were followed by discussion sessions with the audience. For example, one audience, consisting of a group of third graders, attended a presentation based on the changes in transportation. Senior adult participants acted out stories concerning streetcar rides and then progressed to the first public school bus wagons, in which all the boys, due to their rowdiness, were required to ride in a back wagon attached to the main vehicle.

Children from the audience were incorporated into the scene with designated seniors. Here, then, we had a combination of creative and informal drama together with audience members moving easily in and out of the action.

A follow-up discussion showed the interest of the students in the topic of transportation and especially school buses. It was during the discussion that an unspoken respect for the experiences of the elderly emerged through the children's questions about other topics. Another advantage, then, to this theatre technique lies in the intergenerational learning experience. Furthermore, oral history theatre supports history lessons given by the teacher.

Oral History Theatre adds the finishing touch of human experience to the lesson.

Besides providing an effective teaching tool for intergenerational learning, Oral History Theatre also benefits senior participants. Atchley (1977) supports the use of memory to improve the thinking process and says:

> There appears to be a greater loss with age in short-term and recent memory than in remote or old memory, and the decline with age in memory function is less for rote memory than for logical memory. As age increases, the retention of things heard becomes increasingly superior to the retention of things seen, and use of both gives better results than the use of either separately.
>
> Bright people are less susceptible to memory loss with increasing age than are their less intelligent counterparts, and some older people escape memory loss altogether. People who exercise their memories tend to maintain both remote and recent memory well into old age (p. 54).

Thus, life review, reminiscence, and Oral History Theatre support the on-going process of living as participants use the opportunity to remember events and as much of the details of those events as possible. The senior adult is also encouraged by the contribution he or she has made to the community through the presentation of oral history scenes.

Another theatre technique that lends itself to the reaffirmation that the elderly are capable of ongoing contributions is the Talking Book Series.

TALKING BOOK SERIES

The Talking Book Series consists of the drawing of pictures from a designated book onto acetate transparency sheets. The drawings are then accompanied by a tape-recorded radio drama version of the story, complete with music and sound effects. The acetate sheets are then shown on a screen via an overhead projector while the tape provides the viewer with the audio portion of the story.

There are several advantages to this type of theatre activity. One is that seniors are given the opportunity to listen to recordings of their vocal expression and thus better understand their vocal patterns and verbal communication. Many senior adults have never heard their voices played on a tape recorder and benefit from listening to their vocal tones and interpretations of characters.

Another advantage is the ability to include both literate and illiterate, handicapped and nonhandicapped seniors in the activity. Those who are unable to read may provide the sound effects and music. Those who are physically handicapped may find one limb that will provide a needed sound to the tape or may be able to act as a production assistant and cue actors.

A third advantage is that this technique also offers visual arts for the senior to work with. Although some seniors shy away from acting, they prefer some form of visual art as an opportunity for participation within the group. The acetate drawings may be traced directly from a book, with seniors applying appropriate colors to the sheets. Special pens may be purchased at art supply stores or business stores. The drama leader found that Scotch 3M-514 Transparency Marking Pens or Staedtler Lumocolor-317 WP 8 Transparency Pens work well for the coloring of transparencies.

All five project sites used *Whistle For Willie* by Ezra Jack Keats (1964) as their Talking Book Series project, but drama groups may elect to make up their own stories and illustrations.

Whistle For Willie is an especially delightful children's book to work with because it contains possibilities for various sound effects, laughter, and it is loved by all children. Thus, senior adults involved in this project were delighted by the opportunities to whistle, bark like dogs, chant rope-jumping jingles, and sing songs at the beginning and end of the tape. Perhaps the biggest satisfaction, however, came from their watching schoolchildren react to their final product. Each project was donated to an elementary school library at or near each site.

The following radio drama script was developed for a Talking Book Series based on Ezra Jack Keats' *Whistle For Willie*:

WHISTLE FOR WILLIE
by Ezra Jack Keats
adapted for Talking Book Series by Patch Clark

(*SFX: Sound of music playing/guitar.*)
                    NARRATOR
This is the story of *Whistle For Willie* by Ezra Jack Keats. Once there was a little boy named Peter and oh, how he wished he could whistle.

PETER
Oh, I wish I could whistle.
(SFX: Sound of Peter trying to whistle.)
NARRATOR
He saw a boy playing with his dog.
(SFX: Sound of boy calling dog in background and whistling for dog to come to him.)
NARRATOR
Whenever the boy whistled, *(SFX: Sound of boy whistling and dog barking.)* the dog ran to him. Peter tried and tried to whistle *(SFX: Sound of Peter trying to whistle.)* but he couldn't. So instead he turned himself around and around. He whirled faster and faster. *(SFX: Sound of feet turning around and around.)*
PETER
Wheeeee . . . . .
NARRATOR
When he stopped, everything turned down and up and up and down and around and around. Peter saw his dog, Willie, coming. Quick as a wink, he hid in an empty carton lying on the sidewalk. *(SFX: Sound of cardboard being moved and scuffling of feet. Dog barks.)*
PETER
Wouldn't it be funny if I whistled? Willie would stop and look all around and try to see who it was.
NARRATOR
Peter tried and tried to whistle. *(SFX: Sound of Peter trying to whistle.)* But he still couldn't. So Willie just walked on. Peter got out of the carton and started home. On his way home he saw some girls skipping rope. *(SFX: Sound of feet skipping rope on pavement.)*
GIRLS
Jack be nimble, Jack be quick.
Jack jumped over the candlestick.
He jumped so fast, he jumped so high,
He never came down 'til the fourth of July.
NARRATOR
He went past the barber shop and other stores.
SHOPKEEPER # 1
Well, hi there, Peter, what are you doin'?
PETER
I'm tryin' to learn how to whistle. Can you teach me?
SHOPKEEPER # 1
Sure, just put your lips together like this and whistle. *(SFX: Sound of a long, clear whistle. Sound of Peter trying to whistle.)*

NARRATOR

Peter went into his house and put on his father's old hat to make himself feel more grown up. He looked into the mirror to practice whistling. (*SFX: Sound of Peter trying to whistle.*) But still no whistle. When his mother saw what he was doing, Peter pretended to be his father.

PETER

I've come home early today, dear. Is Peter here?

MOTHER

(*Laughing.*) Why, no. He's outside with Willie.

PETER

Well, I'll go look for them.

NARRATOR

Peter went outside and walked along a crack in the sidewalk. He met another shopkeeper.

SHOPKEEPER # 2

Hello, Peter, how are you today?

PETER

I'm trying to learn how to whistle. Can you teach me?

SHOPKEEPER # 2

Sure. Just put your lips together and go like this. (*SFX: Sound of a long, loud whistle.*)

NARRATOR

But Peter tried and tried, (*SFX: Sound of Peter trying to whistle.*) and still couldn't whistle. He came to the corner where the carton was and soon he saw Willie. Peter scrambled under the carton. (*SFX: Sound of Peter crawling under the cardboard carton.*) He blew and blew and blew. (*SFX: Sound of Peter trying to whistle.*) Suddenly, out came a real whistle. (*SFX: Sound of a long, clear whistle.*) Willie stopped and looked around to see who it was.

PETER

It's me! (*SFX: Sound of Willie barking.*)

NARRATOR

Willie raced straight toward Peter. Peter ran home to show his father and mother what he could do.

FATHER

Why, Peter, that's wonderful!

MOTHER

Good for you, Peter!

NARRATOR

They loved Peter's whistling and so did Willie. (*SFX: Sound of Peter whistling and Willie barking.*) THE END!

THEATRE TECHNIQUES / 127

Whistle For Willie

Seniors Prepare Artwork

The various talents of participants located at sites A and E added unique components to the Talking Book Project. A blind guitar player at Site A provided the introductory music, and several participants at Site E devised creative methods of producing sound effects. Some brought wood blocks from home to produce the sound of girls skipping rope, and others found cardboard that, combined with a rubbing motion against various surfaces, provided the sound of Peter hiding underneath the cardboard box.

Participants were encouraged to devise their own methods of sound effects and each site selected their own music. Everyone had a specific assignment and took on their tasks with great seriousness. Involvement in this project also produced a new activity within several of the sites--whistling.

The reaction of the child audience to the finished project was very enthusiastic and the senior participants were especially proud and delighted while watching the children become absorbed in the story.

The involvement of children as audience members and finally as active participants brought about the development of Intergenerational Participatory Theatre, yet another technique that helped to explore and develop the talents of senior adults at each of the sites.

INTERGENERATIONAL PARTICIPATORY THEATRE

Participatory theatre is closely related to creative dramatics in that it offers participants creative experiences that are non-threatening in design, and it reinforces the individual talents of each group member. Intergenerational participatory theatre, involving various age groups, may be divided into three categories: (1) participatory historical theatre; (2) fill-in-the-blank participatory theatre; and (3) participatory storybook theatre.

Participatory Historical Theatre

Participatory historical theatre involves the research and writing of a story that centers on a specific event. A designated storyteller acts as the narrator while participants become the characters and interject dialogue throughout the production. No rehearsal process is necessary unless the group decides to produce this as formal theatre, in which case the production may be embellished with scenery, props, costumes, or lights, depending upon how complex the group wishes to make the final product.

The following story was developed and used both as a creative drama exercise and as an intergenerational experience with children involved in the story. Teachers, parents, and senior adults act as family members with children acting as grandchildren, horses, or, depending upon the age and desire of the child, various characters in the story.

CANAL BOATS

Characters
Captain Sam Wyatt
Canal boat stewards
Mothers, fathers, uncles, aunts, grandparents
Horses
Ticket taker
Narrator

Possible Props
Sailor's hats made from newspapers
Captain's hat (either borrowed or constructed)
Tickets (made from construction paper)
Baggage (book bags, sacks, boxes)

NARRATOR
Once upon a time in a place called Richmond, Virginia, there were several canal boats which ran up and down the James River. (*Participants who are playing the horses leading the canal boats begin to make a circle around the room. Captain Sam Wyatt stands in the middle of the circle observing the imaginary waters.*) What a bustle there was at the foot of Eighth Street when someone yelled, (*Narrator designates one of the passengers for this line and whispers line for Passenger to yell out.*)

PASSENGER
Trahnn-ahnnnn up the canal! Trahnn-ahnnnn up the canal!

NARRATOR
Children, parents, aunts and uncles, grandparents, everyone came running to board the canal boat. (*The Narrator leads the passengers to a designated area of the room and positions the Ticket-Takers. Passengers begin to board the boat as the present their tickets and form a line behind Captain Sam.*) Some were going to see their relatives and friends in Lynchburg and others to finish business. The baggage was stored up on the top deck. (*Passen-

gers pass imaginary baggage to be stored to the stewards.) And stewards ran hither and thither inquiring,

STEWARD

(*Again, the Narrator may prompt the character.*) How is your health, sir? And yours, madam?

NARRATOR

The boat was slowly pushed off at five miles an hour, and it slid under the bridge at Seventh Street before being hitched to the towpath horses. (*Steward may pantomime the securing of the horses.*) Suddenly, the boat jerked. (*Participants respond physically to this.*) The horses broke into a trot. ("*Horses*" *do so travelling in a circle around Captain Sam. Passengers, Stewards, and Ticket Takers fall in line behind the horses and travel in a circle.*) The canal boat went up the river at eight miles an hour with the great paddle wheels turning as fast as they could go. (*If there are participants who are also observers, they may make the motion for the wheels, or perhaps some of the actors in the story might provide this motion.*) Captain Sam Wyatt stood on the deck with his feet apart and smoked his pipe. (*Captain Sam does so.*) At one point along the trip, the Captain would call out,

CAPTAIN SAM

Loooow Bridge!!!! Loooow Bridge!!!

NARRATOR

And everyone knew they had to duck. (*Participants all duck as Wyatt calls out command.*) But one day somebody forgot to duck and into the river they went! (*Designated person does so.*) What a commotion! . . . people running and yelling everywhere.

PASSENGERS

(*Ad-libbed*) Toss some rope! Help! Help! man . . . woman . . . person overboard!

NARRATOR

And everyone rushed to one side of the boat while the stewards helped the person back on board. (*Stewards do so and passengers applaud.*) Captain Sam Wyatt called out again,

CAPTAIN SAM

Lynchburg landing! Lynchburg landing!

NARRATOR

Everyone scurried to get their baggage and the children waved goodbye to the Captain. (*Children and families do so. Horses stop and Stewards help Passengers collect baggage and disembark. Offstage observers might serve as the relatives and friends waiting on the banks to greet the Passengers.*) . . . and that's generally how it went when there were canal boats along the James River.

EVERYONE

The End!

THEATRE TECHNIQUES / 131

Canal Boats: Making Props

Canal Boats: The Ticket Taker

This particular story was used in various ways according to the needs of the participants at each of the sites. Sites A and E involved the children from the elementary school and their teachers. Site D scheduled a special drama event day and the *Canal Boat* story was one of many dramas the children experienced that day. Sites B and C used this particular story as part of their creative drama experiences and training.

At all sites, the follow-up discussion was of great importance to those involved. Usually the story would spur memories of early transportation and, thus, discussions of changes in transportation would follow. And although this particular story refers specifically to Richmond, Virginia, the story was adapted to Washington, D.C., and the Georgetown Canals, or sometimes, participants would recall other regions where canal boats were used.

The success of this theatre technique is carried over to yet another participatory exercise, Fill-in-the-Blank Participatory Theatre.

Fill-In-the-Blank Participatory Theatre

In this particular exercise, participants are given a story that contains missing words. The participants decide upon the words to complete the story and an exaggerated movement to accompany each word. In some cases, the senior adults had already prepared the story and taught the children the words and movements on the day of the presentation. In other instances children and senior participants worked together in deciding upon words and movements. A copy of the following incomplete story was distributed to each participant:

CREATE YOUR OWN TITLE

One hot summer day in a nearby town called _____, the townspeople decided to have a celebration. Now, they decided to have a celebration because it was so hot and miserable in the town of _____ that all the townspeople could do was sit around and say, _____.

Now, in this town of _____, where all the people were sitting around saying _____ there lived a nearby wealthy mayor whose name was _____ and all he could say was _____ .

Well, when the Mayor whose name was _____ came to the meeting place of the town called _____ he was very surprised to hear the townspeople singing the song _____ instead of saying _____ as they usually did. This made the Mayor, whose name was _____ very happy and because he was so happy he decided to give the townspeople of _____ a huge _____.

Well the townspeople of _____ were so happy to receive this _____ that they never again sat around saying _____, but instead sang the song _____ and had a wonderful celebration.
THE END

Fill-in-the-Blank Participatory Theatre:
One Hot Summer Day . . .

In one instance, the senior adults had just returned from a shopping trip in Georgetown. Although they had enjoyed this outing, many complained of the high prices and were frustrated by the limitations of their fixed incomes. The following story served as a positive outlet through which to voice their opinions:

GEORGETOWN

One hot summer day in a nearby town called *Georgetown* (make large rounded movement with arms each time *Georgetown* is repeated) the townspeople decided to have a celebration. Now, they decided to have a celebration because it was so hot in *Georgetown* that all the townspeople could do was sit around and say, "*I'm going down and get dressed up!*" (Each time townspeople say this line, say with anger. Movement--hands on hips.)

Well, in this town of *Georgetown* where all the townspeople were sitting around saying, "*I'm going down and get dressed up*," there lived a nearby wealthy mayor and his name was *Tom*. (Each time *Tom* is said, pantomime large fat man with a cigar). All he and his wife could say was, "*Look around. We have nice things.*" (Make gesture as if to hold up merchandise).

Well, when *Tom* and his wife came to the meeting place of the town called *Georgetown*, they were very surprised to hear the townspeople singing the song *Good night, Georgetown, Goodnight, Georgetown, Goodnight, Georgetown, we're going to leave you now*, (march in a line around the room), instead of saying, "*I'm going down and get dressed up*," as they usually did.

This made *Tom* and his wife very upset so he decided to give the people of *Georgetown* a huge DISCOUNT (participants cheer and Mayor and wife hold up signs saying PRICES REDUCED).

The people of *Georgetown* were so happy to receive this DISCOUNT that they never again sat around saying, "*I'm going down and get dressed up*," but sang the song, *Hello, Georgetown, hello, Georgetown, hello, Georgetown, we're going to buy some things*! And had a wonderful celebration!

THE END

In this particular presentation, participants made signs, wore a variety of hats as costumes, and added the character of the Mayor's wife. An area of the room was designated as the "shopping area" and the Mayor and his wife were given bright red sashes to drape across their shoulders and chest to give them a royal appearance.

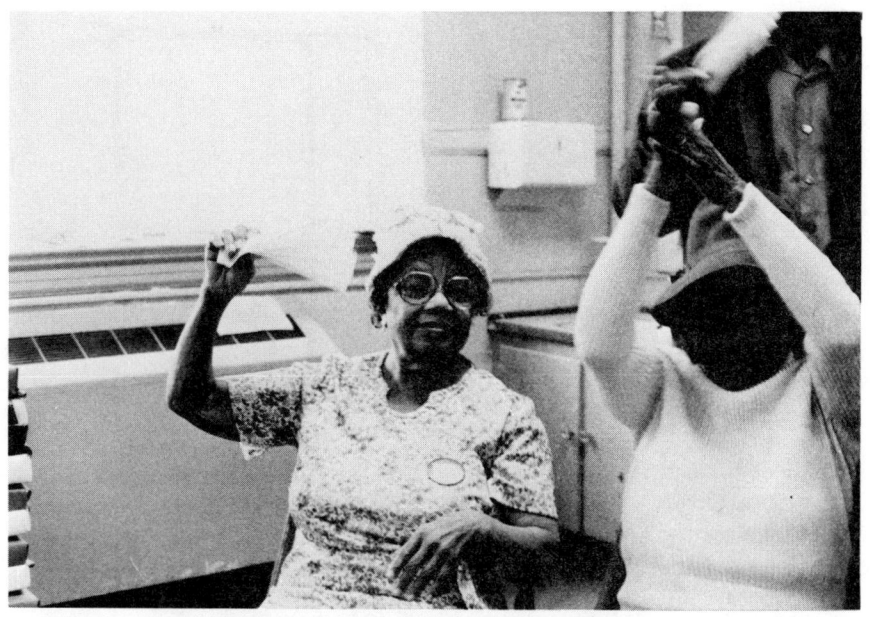

Fill-in-the-Blank Participatory Theatre:
In a Nearby Town Called....

There was much laughter and kidding as senior participants prepared the story and invented movements. They enjoyed making the presentation to the children and the discussion that followed explored the topic of inflation. Thus, this particular fill-in-the-blank exercise served three purposes: (1) as a therapeutic outlet; (2) as an intergenerational theatre experience; and (3) as a stimulus for discussion of price changes in history.

One final intergenerational-participatory theatre technique used at all five sites was that of Participatory Storybook Theatre.

Participatory Storybook Theatre

Participatory Storybook Theatre involves the children and senior adults in the creation and selection of popular children's books and stories. The selected stories are then acted out with individual members playing various characters from the original story. Inexpensive or borrowed props and costumes become a part of the exercise and children may work together with their senior partners in the construction of these added affects.

Participatory Storybook Theatre

At all five sites, original stories were created and books selected for the purpose of dramatization. One of the most popular books selected for this intergenerational experience was *Emma*, by Wendy Kesselman. The following checklist was used in the final selection process:

Checklist -- Book Dramatization

____ Is the book recommended by either the teacher or the school librarian?
____ Are the characters well-defined and easily adaptable for dramatization?

_____ Is the plot well constructed and easily adaptable for dramatization?
_____ Are there a sufficient number of characters to accommodate the number of participants in the group?
_____ Do children enjoy the book?
_____ Do the senior adults enjoy the book?
_____ Does the book contain possibilities for the construction of props, costumes, and other added effects?
_____ Is there physical action?
_____ Does the plot lend itself to intergenerational interaction?
_____ Does the plot contain possibilities for music and/or dance?

The author of *Emma*, Wendy Kesselman, is familiar with the problems of aging and family relationships and has written plays for children, as well. Her intergenerational play, *Maggie-Magalita*, winner of the Sharfman Playwriting Competition, was produced at the Kennedy Center in 1980. It is because of Kesselman's talent as a playwright and depth of understanding as a person that the story of *Emma* lends itself so successfully to intergenerational dramatization.

EMMA
by Wendy Kesselman
adapted for dramatization by Patch Clark and Wendy Kesselman

Pre-Production Activities

o   Read the story of *Emma* to children and senior adults.
o   Discuss important points made in the story.
o   Ask the question, "Could this story actually happen?"
o   Explain to the group that Emma was a real person whom the author of the story knew.
o   Ask if any of the participants have pets.
o   Ask if any of the senior adult participants have specific memories of their homeland, original home, etc.
o   Provide participants with art materials such as construction paper, drawing paper, glue, scissors, tape, paints.

- o Ask participants to draw pictures of their pets and their homes or homelands (these will later be used as Emma's paintings in the dramatization).
- o Provide participants with boxes and wrapping paper; ask participants to wrap them as birthday present props for the dramatization.

EMMA

Characters
Emma, the 72-year-old grandmother
Pumpkinseed, her faithful cat
Delivery person, may be any age
Family, four children, seven grandchildren, fourteen great-grandchildren (the number of family members may be changed according to the number of participants)

NARRATOR
It was Emma's birthday. She was 72 years old. (*Family members begin to file in with gifts.*) Emma had four children, seven grandchildren, and fourteen great-grandchildren.
FAMILY MEMBERS
(*Singing*) Happy birthday to you, happy birthday to you, happy birthday, dear Emma, happy birthday to you! (*Family gathers around a table.*)
NARRATOR
Emma was happy when her family came to visit. She baked noodle puddings and chocolate cream pies. She put flowers everywhere.
EMMA'S DAUGHTER
Oh, Emma, you always have such pretty flowers.
NARRATOR
Her family brought her lots of presents, but never stayed very long.
EMMA'S GREAT-GRANDSON
We brought you some presents, Grandma.
EMMA'S SON
But we can't stay, Emma. We have to go.
EMMA
Oh, thank you. (*She begins to open the presents. Seeing the family getting ready to leave.*) Oh, but can't you stay a little bit longer?

EMMA'S DAUGHTER
No, we've got to run now. (*The Family begins filing out the door, waving and yelling goodbyes.*) (*Emma sinks down in her chair.*)
NARRATOR
So most of the time Emma was all alone. And sometimes she was very lonely. The only company she had was her orange cat, Pumpkinseed. (*Pumpkinseed enters and rubs up against Emma.*) They sat outside together and curled their toes in the sun. (*Child holds up a huge construction paper sun while Emma and Pumpkinseed pantomime going outside. Another child holds up branches around a chair to become a tree.*) They listened to the woodpecker tapping at the old apple tree. (*Either a senior adult or a child makes this sound.*) Sometimes Pumpkinseed got stuck at the top of the tree, (*Pumpkinseed climbs up in the "tree-chair."*) and Emma had to climb up and rescue him. (*Emma reaches her arms in an upward movement and pantomimes "rescuing her cat."*) But Emma didn't mind. She loved climbing trees. (*Pumpkinseed and Emma go back into the "house." Emma sits in her chair with Pumpkinseed at her feet.*)

She loved all kinds of simple things. She loved to see the snow come right up to her doorstep. (*Family members who are now located together in a different part of the space make the sound of a blizzard: Oooooooooooooo, Oooooooooooooo!*) She loved to sit and dream about the little village across the mountains where she grew up. But when she told her family about the things she loved, they laughed and said to each other,
EMMA'S SON
(*Standing up or taking the focus in some way.*) Poor Emma. She must be getting old! (*Family members laugh.*)
NARRATOR
For her 72nd birthday the family gave Emma a painting of her little village across the mountains. She hung the painting on the wall, and though she had told them it was beautiful, she thought to herself,
EMMA
(*Emma pulling back a curtain or placing this painting on an easel.*) That's not how I remember my village at all.
NARRATOR
Every day Emma looked at the painting and frowned. And every day her frown grew a little deeper. (*Emma frowns.*) One day Emma decided,
EMMA
That's it! I've made up my mind!

NARRATOR

She called the art store.

DELIVERY BOY

Knock knock! Anybody home? (*Pulling out paints and brushes.*) I've got these paints, and brushes, and . . . are *you* the one who called for these? (*Looking curiously at Emma.*)

EMMA

I'm the one! I've been waiting for these for ages.

NARRATOR

Then Emma sat by the window and painted her village just the way she remembered it. When it was finished she took the other painting off the wall and hung hers up instead. (*Emma switches the paintings.*) And every day Emma looked at her painting and smiled. (*Emma smiles.*)

When her family came to visit, Emma put the other painting back again.

EMMA'S GRANDSON

Knock, knock, knock! It's me, Gran'ma Emma. I've come for a visit.

EMMA

Oh, Dear. Oh, Dear. Wait a minute! Just a minute! (*She scurries about and switches the painting, then opens the imaginary door.*) Ohhh, I'm so glad you came. (*They hug.*)

EMMA'S GRANDSON

Well, I can't stay. I just came to say hello.

EMMA

Oh, stay awhile and have something to eat.

EMMA'S GRANDSON

Sorry, Grandma, I gotta run now. (*He runs off. Emma switches the paintings.*)

NARRATOR

And as soon as they left she switched it for her own. (*There is a pause.*) But one day Emma forgot.

EMMA'S FAMILY

(*The family begins to file in with "hello's" and hugs and sits around a table.*) Hello, Emma, we've come to eat.

NARRATOR

When the family was in the middle of dinner, one of Emma's grandchildren pointed to the wall.

EMMA'S GRANDCHILD

Where did that painting come from? It's not the one we gave you!

NARRATOR

Emma looked up. Emma looked down. But everyone kept right on looking at the painting and they all kept asking,

EMMA'S FAMILY
(*Ad-lib.*) It's not the one we gave you. Where's the one we gave you? Yeah, where is it, Emma?
EMMA'S GRANDSON
Yes, where did that painting come from?
NARRATOR
Finally Emma said,
EMMA
Me. (*Very softly.*) I did it.
EMMA'S FAMILY
You!
NARRATOR
Emma hurried to hide the painting in the closet.
EMMA'S DAUGHTER
Stop! Don't hide it away!
EMMA'S GRANDCHILDREN
AND GREAT-GRANDCHILDREN
It's beautiful!
EMMA'S SON
Why don't you paint another?
EMMA
I have.
NARRATOR
And she brought 20 more paintings out of the closet. (*Emma passes the paintings around to each of the family members. As the narrator describes each of the paintings, family members stand up at the table and show the audience each painting.*) From that day Emma kept painting and she never stopped. (*Emma sits at her easel and paints.*) She painted the snow coming right up to her doorstep. (*Family member shows painting.*) She painted the old apple tree in blossom with the woodpecker tapping at its branches. (*Family member shows painting.*) She painted Pumpkinseed curling his toes in the sun. (*Family member shows painting and Pumpkinseed lets out a loud "Meow!" of approval.*) And she painted her village across the mountains over and over and over again. (*Family members stand and show village paintings.*)
NARRATOR
Soon, people began coming from everywhere to look at Emma's paintings. (*Remaining family members become various dignitaries who have come to look at the paintings.*) When they left, she was all alone. (*Family members secure paintings to the wall of the room and exit.*) But now Emma had something else. She sat by the window every day and painted from morning (*Child holds up sun.*) till night. (*Senior adult holds up moon.*)

She painted hundreds of paintings. Her paintings covered the walls. They filled the closets. They hung in the kitchen cupboards. Emma was surrounded by the friends and places she loved. And she was never lonely again.

PUMPKINSEED

(*Curling up beside Emma contentedly.*) Meow!

THE END

The dramatization of *Emma* closely resembles formal play production. Because there is a script and dialogue that must be conveyed to the audience, it is necessary to cast appropriate people in the various roles. The narrator may use a script bound in an attractive cover. The dramatization may take several rehearsals; thus this particular storybook theatre project may continue for several sessions.

The drama leader found that both seniors and children learned dialogue quickly after three rehearsal sessions. The script was divided into three segments to aid in the learning of dialogue and story sequence. Segment one began with the first line spoken by the narrator and ended with Emma's Son's line, "Poor Emma. She must be getting old." Segment two began with the Narrator's line, "For her 72nd birthday . . . ," and ended with the Narrator's line, ". . . but one day Emma forgot." Segment three began with Emma's family entering and saying, "Hello, Emma, we've come to eat," and ended with Pumpkinseed's final "Meow."

Children and Seniors

The response to *Emma* was very positive and school librarians reported that children requested the book to take home to read and act out for their parents.

Upon experiencing success in storybook theatre, senior participants expressed an interest in writing original scripts. Two of the five sites completed original scripts (See Appendix) and held special performances for the community. Their enthusiasm for writing original material led to several sessions in playwriting techniques. The drama leader found that those who were interested in writing discovered new talents and added confidence as they concentrated on Original Scriptwriting.

ORIGINAL SCRIPTWRITING

The participants involved in the playwriting process had not had previous experience in writing but by this time had had experience in creative drama, oral history theatre, participatory theatre, and a very brief introduction to classical dramatic literature.

They had specific messages they wished to convey to an audience and expressed an interest in having the senior adult drama groups present special performances for their families, friends, and colleagues at the sites.

Lunch at the White House Cast Members

144 / SENIORS ON STAGE

At one site, the script revolved around several oral history stories and at the second the playwright was interested in writing a comedy concerning the administration and visiting dignitaries at the White House.

A Senior Actor-Playwright Takes a Break

The drama leader began by using improvisational theatre techniques with the group to develop possible dialogue. The participants were accustomed to this technique because they had already experienced the Who, What, Where technique. In searching for ideas for scene development, however, the playwright now functioned as the director of the improvisational scenework.

IMPROVISATIONAL SCENEWORK AS A MODE FOR PLAYWRITING

Up until this point, the seniors had experienced only that improvisational scenework that contained the Who, What, and Where information. A more advanced method is the assignment of a director who at any point during the course of the scene may call out the following directives to the actors in the scene:

FREEZE!

1. Go to the future (be specific about *how* far into the future).
2. Go to the past (be specific about *how* far into the past).
3. Add a subplot (tell the actors *what* the subplot concerns).
4. Add a character (tell the actors *who* the character is and *what* he is doing).
5. Exit a character (tell which character should exit).
6. Add a twist in the plot (tell what the twist should be).
7. Develop an ending.
8. Develop a surprise ending.

It is through this exercise that the actors and the director/playwright discover ideas for characters, dialogue, and scene development. The director/playwrights were asked to write down any pertinent lines they felt they might use in their plays. Other members of the group were enthusiastic about making suggestions and excited about the final results.

The drama leader also gave the playwrights the following guidelines to use in the creation of their scripts:

1. Observe characters from life and use their mannerisms, speech patterns, personalities, idiosyncracies, whatever seems appropriate for the purpose of your play.
2. Characters should be well defined, regardless of whether they have one line to say or 100 lines.
3. The plot should develop in a believable manner, even if the play is based upon fantasy. The audience should believe the action is actually taking place.
4. Develop a plot so that there is a turning point or climax.
5. Ask yourself, "What is the theme of my script?"
6. Ask yourself, "Has this script made a point either through the action or through the characterizations?"
7. Ask yourself, "Do I feel I know these characters?"

Although playwriting is a sophisticated process that reaches beyond answering questions, observing people, and developing improvisational scenework, this introduction proved adequate for the playwright's immediate purposes. It is hoped that these seniors are continuing to write and are advancing their talents and techniques.

Their efforts were met with overwhelming applause, and they were very proud of their final product. They filled a new role in the drama group, that of playwrights in residence.

By the close of the ten-month period, the senior drama groups became known by the community and respected by family members, site directors, colleagues, and teachers. The once "vacant aesthetic space," was now filled with memories of characters, scenes, songs, words, poetry, music, dance, sounds, drawings, friendships, laughter, and fun. The space had been transformed into an aesthetic environment.

Sometimes, however, there were obstacles to overcome. Those obstacles included the handicapping conditions of some of the participants and the efforts of the group to meet the challenge of incorporating these participants into the groups' activities.

In Chapter 6 some of the specific techniques used at all five sites are discussed. These techniques were integrated into the regular drama program and added only to our building of an aesthetic space.

REFERENCES

Atchley, R. 1977. *The Social Forces in Later Life.* Belmont, California: Wadsworth Publishing.
Chayefsky, Paddy. 1954. "The Mother." In *Best Television Plays*, edited by Gore Vidal. New York: Ballantine Books.
Guthrie Theatre. 1978-79. "Flashbacks: A Scrapbook of Personal Portraits." Mimeographed sheet. Minneapolis: The Guthrie Theatre, Outreach Programming.
Hagen, U. 1973. *Respect for Acting.* New York: Macmillan.
Jerome, J. 1974. *The Poet and the Poem.* Cincinnati: Writer's Digest Books.
Keats, E. 1964. *Whistle for Willie.* New York: The Viking Press.
Kernodle, G. and P. Kernodle. 1978. *Invitation to the Theatre* 2nd ed. New York: Harcourt Brace, Jovanovich.
Kesselman, Wendy. 1980. *Emma.* New York: Doubleday.
More, V. 1943. *Virginia Is a State of Mind.* New York: E. P. Dutton.
Spolin, V. 1976. *Improvisations for the Theatre.* Evanston, Illinois: Northwestern University Press.
Stanislavski, C. 1949. *Building A Character.* Translated by Elizabeth Reynolds Hapgood. New York: Theatre Arts Books.
____. 1961. *Creating A Role.* Translated by Elizabeth Reynolds Hapgood. New York: Theatre Arts Books.

6

APPLIED THEATRE TECHNIQUES WITH THE HANDICAPPED ELDERLY

It is unusual to hear the expression "gifted handicapped." It is a contradiction of terms. This paradox, however, is included in the title of Maker's book *Providing Programs for the Gifted Handicapped* (1977) in which she states:

> Educators have long talked about the uniqueness of each individual and about each individual's particular strengths and weaknesses. A person who is handicapped and gifted should not be a stranger. That person simply has *both* strengths and weaknesses that are very pronounced (p. 7).

Whereas physical handicaps may be easy to identify, emotional and intellectual impairments may sometimes be difficult to recognize. A further complication concerns the division between art for the sake of artistry and art for the sake of therapy, for there exist some therapeutic qualities in all art forms.

Therapeutic art can be further divided into dance, drama, music and the visual arts. Each field has developed training and certification programs that enable specialists to provide qualified guidance for the handicapped participant.

In working with senior adults at the five experimental sites, the drama leader, assisted by the site directors, was able to identify four handicapped participants. Two of the participants were physically handicapped, and the other two had been involved in psychological counseling for depression.

The leader's primary objective was to encourage successful social reintegration through positive experiences in a drama group. Furthermore, in an effort to alleviate possible discriminatory practices, applied theatre techniques were incorporated into the regular drama program. Thus, the handicapped and nonhandicapped worked together, with their primary objectives focused on completion or involvement in a drama exercise rather than on any individual handicapping condition. The result was the volunteering of several of the nonhandicapped members of the group to assist those who were handicapped. The final focus became that of the group's drama project and the handicapped participants no longer felt "left out," "different," or "unwanted." They felt more confident and purposeful.

Music, movement, dance, and the visual arts became important motivating tools in this successful reintegration of the handicapped individuals. The integration of the various arts proved vital to the implementation of the applied theatre techniques for the handicapped.

MUSIC ACTIVITIES AS AN APPLIED THEATRE TECHNIQUE

One of the participants had been without his sight since the age of three. Fortunately, someone also handed him a guitar, and (we will refer to him as *Mr. Sam*) Mr. Sam had developed his gift for music. Mr. Sam was mobile with the aide of a cane, but was usually isolated from the rest of the participants. Though the others were friendly and polite to him, he did not have a group at the site with which he conversed and shared his meals.

He was invited to join the drama group and, after some hesitation, agreed to attend on a trial basis.

Mr. Sam's "trial basis" extended through the duration of the program and he provided the group with musical interludes for the talking book series, songs for the participatory children's theatre, and finally, when we were tired of rehearsals or needed some extra motivation, Mr. Sam sat and played his guitar while we sang just for enjoyment.

Mr. Sam's "gift" to the group was his musical talent, and as he became more involved in the drama projects he developed more friendships within the group and was thought of as a valued artist and companion. The seniors developed some of the following techniques to aid Mr. Sam's active involvement in the drama program:

1. The assignment of a "seeing-scenepartner" to walk with the blind participant through participatory theatre.
2. The development of special characters who always stayed together, thus justifying Mr. Sam's "seeing-scenepartner."
3. The entire group always made certain that Mr. Sam was handed costumes to feel before putting them on. We described the colors to him.
4. In participatory theatre we developed a "stage walk-around" to enable Mr. Sam to count the number of steps and establish space relationships.
5. Mr. Sam's "seeing-scenepartner" worked out physical cues--for example, a touch on the right elbow meant that he had to turn right--to aid in the movement in a scene.
6. We described the visual images used in the talking book series to aid in Mr. Sam's understanding of the total project and how his music might be integrated.
7. We explained to the children that Mr. Sam could not see and discussed with them the various techniques we were using to ensure his safety during participatory theatre. (Interestingly, *all* of the children wanted to be Mr. Sam's "seeing-scene-partner.")

Mr. Sam's talent in music helped in his successful social reintegration. Furthermore, he was able to apply his talent to specific projects; the absence of such channels in the past had prevented him from fully exploring his musical abilities. His obvious contribution to the group gave him a feeling of purpose and his final response at the end of the program was, "I didn't know I could 'see' so much!"

Other musical activities were incorporated into the drama program at various times. The following are applied-theatre music techniques that were successfully used at each of the five sites.

Musical Parts

All participants sit in chairs and close their eyes. The drama leader plays a recording (see Appendix for suggestions). Objective: To increase listening skills and encourage physical movement.

1. Players are instructed to move fingers as they listen to the music.

2. Players are instructed to move arms and fingers.
3. Players are instructed to stop movement and listen.
4. Players are instructed to move toes.
5. Players are instructed to move toes and legs.
6. Players are instructed to stop movement and listen.
7. Players are instructed to breathe in and out and focus on breathing patterns while listening to music.
8. Players are instructed to move head while listening to music.
9. Players are instructed to stop movement and listen to the music.
10. Players are instructed to move torso as they listen to music.
11. Players are instructed to stop movement and imagine they are moving to the music.
12. Players are instructed to move any part of the body.
13. Players are instructed to move any part of the body with eyes open.

Adaptation for Hearing Impaired. Drama leader or "hearing-partner" sits opposite hearing impaired participant and indicates the rhythm of the music by making a motion using hands or other parts of the body. Drama leader may hold up preprinted signs that give visual instructions.

Musical Characters

All participants sit in chairs. The drama leader plays a recording (see Appendix for suggestions). Objective: To identify various rhythms as the basis for characterization. Supplies: Large posterboard with various examples of characters: A mother, a king, a plumber, a circus performer, or so forth.

1. Participants are instructed to listen to the music.
2. Participants are instructed to move to the music.
3. Participants are instructed to listen to the music and think of a character they feel the music best suggests.
4. Each participant takes a turn moving as his or her character without the music.
5. Each participant moves as his character with the music.
6. Participants are asked to choose a character from the list on the posterboard and move to the music as that character would move.

TECHNIQUES WITH THE HANDICAPPED / 151

Adaptation for Hearing Impaired. Drama leader or "hearing-partner" sits opposite hearing impaired participant and indicates the rhythm of the music. Drama leader holds up preprinted signs that give visual instructions.

Adaptation for Visually Impaired. Drama leader reads aloud the character choices. Visually impaired participant holds the hand, arm, or shoulders of other participants as they move to the music.

Musical Emotions

All participants sit in chairs. Objective: To identify various emotions suggested by the melodies and rhythms in music. Supplies: Either cards with various emotions written on them, or pictures of people or drawings of facial expressions that indicate such emotions as happiness, sadness, loneliness, fright, surprise, or anger.

1. Participants are given three cards at a time.
2. Drama leader plays music and participants are asked to hold up cards that they feel correspond with the music. The rhythms may change and they are asked to make these changes accordingly.

Adaptation for Hearing Impaired. Drama leader or "hearing-partner" sits opposite hearing impaired partner and indicates the rhythm of the music. Hearing partner may make facial expressions that indicate emotions and hearing impaired participant holds up corresponding card.

Adaptation for Visually Impaired. Visually impaired participant makes his or her own faces instead of using cards. For projects that have access to funding, papier mâché masks can be constructed that indicate various emotions and the visually impaired participant may hold these up.

Found Sounds

Everyone in the group participates. Objective: To discover objects in the room that may be used as musical instruments.

1. Participants are asked to travel around the room and experiment by listening to tapping on a chair, opening and

closing a door, clicking a pen, or any other noises they might make with found objects within the room.
2. Drama leader plays a recording while participants listen.
3. Drama leader instructs participants to select one "found sound" as their musical instrument.
4. Drama leader plays the recording again while tapping out the dominant rhythm.
5. Each participant "plays" his or her "found sound" instrument for the rest of the group.
6. The drama leader plays the recording and participants play their "found sounds" along with the recording.
7. The group plays their "found sounds" without the recording while either the drama leader or one of the participants conducts the "found sound orchestra."

Adaptation for Hearing Impaired. Drama leader assigns the role of conductor to hearing impaired participant. The "conductor" holds up large circles of different colored construction paper (one at a time) and the "orchestra" is instructed to "play" their found sound according to the conductor's color. Red may indicate loud, blue may indicate soft, etc.

The hearing impaired participant may also become a part of the orchestra through the help of an assigned musical partner who shows the rhythm and assists in the selection of a found sound. The hearing impaired participant can feel the rhythm of the sound as he or she makes the movement.

Adaptation for Visually Impaired. Drama leader assigns the role of "conductor" to the visually impaired. If the visually impaired participant can hear, the remainder of the exercise remains the same. The only difficulty might be in following a conductor; thus, the assignment of this participant as the conductor will alleviate this problem.

Once participants became comfortable with listening and moving to music they felt more confident about approaching dance. Their involvement in music activities had helped them to become less physically self-conscious thus less inhibited and more creative in their movements. The progression, then, came naturally, as the seniors discovered yet another avenue for creative expression through dance-movement exercises.

DANCE-MOVEMENT ACTIVITIES AS AN APPLIED THEATRE TECHNIQUE

> I used to dance. I used to love to dance. I'd dance all
> night long, just twirling around and around. I wish I
> could still do that . . . dance like I used to.

So sighed the old woman in a wheelchair. For some, the memories of dancing are positive, for others, even the mention of the word *dance* presents a threat. But to be able to enjoy one's own movement to the sound of a rhythm, to the beating of a drum, is one of the greatest of all pleasures. We all carry with us personal physical rhythms that communicate melodies of emotions. When we are angry our body changes and our physical rhythms and gestures perform different manners than, say, when we are quiet, relaxed, and thoughtful.

The physical release of emotions has been recognized for its therapeutic values by many and especially by those involved in the field of dance therapy. As Anderson states, "The basic idea of dance therapy is that body movement is a natural medium of self-expression and communication--a capacity that becomes impaired, to some extent, in all of us--and that an expanded ability to move the body can also be an expansion and reintegration of the whole personality" (1977, p. 56).

For the senior adult involved in dance-movement activities this may mean a gradual reintegration because many, though there has been a renewed interest in exercise for the elderly, are not involved in physical activities. Consequently, the drama leader integrated dance-movement exercises into the regular drama program gradually, beginning with music activities and movement to music as discussed earlier in this chapter.

Several of the music exercises, such as Musical Parts, Musical Characters, and Musical Emotions, were reintroduced, but participants were asked to move about the room rather than stay stationary in their chairs. The following dance exercises were then introduced at each of the sites.

Scarf-Chairdancing

The full group participates in this activity. Objective: To introduce participants to dance through an object as an extension of their own movement. Supplies: Long scarves, sheer fabric, or material that is lightweight and will flow when waved in the air.

1. Participants are asked to select a scarf from a box.
2. Participants sit in chairs in a large circle.
3. Participants listen to a recording (see Appendix for suggestions).
4. Participants are asked to move the scarves while listening to the music.
5. Drama leader gives movement commands such as "high"--participants wave scarves above their heads--"low"--participants move scarves in a lowered position--"fast," "slow," "circles," "wave to the person next to you," "wave to the person across from you," "wave to anybody."
6. Participants are asked to assume an emotion as they move the scarves.
7. Participants are asked to create a character with the scarf. They may drape the scarves around themselves, tie them on their heads, tie them around their waists, etc.
8. Participants are asked to stand and move around the room while listening to the music and to use their scarves as parts of "character" costumes.
9. Each participant is asked to find a partner and share a scarf.
10. Participants are asked to assist each other in moving the scarves.
11. Participants are asked to move in pairs around the room while listening to the music.

Adaptation for Physically Impaired. Drama leader asks entire group to tie their scarves around their heads and move to the music (if the physically impaired participant has use of the head), or they are to tie the scarves around their arms, legs, or whatever appendage the handicapped person has use of. The scarf may even be held between the teeth, if necessary, to include handicapped participants.

One participant tied a scarf to each side of her wheelchair and, while being pushed around the room by a dance partner, held the scarves out to create a flowing movement.

Rhythm-Movement Master

The full group participates. Objective: To introduce participants to physical interpretations of various rhythms.

Scarf-Chairdancing

1. Participants may either sit or move about the room.
2. One participant is designated as the "Rhythm-Movement Master" and is given a drum, wood blocks, or improvised instrument with which to beat out a rhythm.
3. As the "Master" begins to beat a rhythm, participants move various parts of the body. When the sound of the rhythm stops, participants maintain their poses.
4. The "Master" passes the rhythm instrument to another participant who then assumes the role of "Master."

Colordance

The full group participated. Objective: To introduce participants to physical interpretations of color. Supplies: Large construction paper circles of various colors.

1. The drama leader or designated participant holds up circles at various times and participants move in response to the color.
2. Participants add music that they feel best represents a color and thus dancers are moving to the sound of color as well. Red may indicate fast movement, green slow and flowing, yellow light, etc.

Adaptation for the Visually Impaired. The drama leader may cue the participant orally as to which color is being held up. If the participant has never seen color, the drama leader may suggest emotions that coincide with the color.

Choreopoem--Dance

All members of the group participate. Objective: To integrate dance, visual arts, and music in a drama exercise. Supplies: Group poem that participants have composed. "Today I feel _____. Yesterday I felt _____. Tomorrow I will feel _____."

1. Participants are asked to select one of the sentences from the group poem and assume a still position.
2. Each participant is then asked to say the selected line and begin to move.
3. Participants may either be placed in a line or given numbers to designate the order in which they speak.

4. Music is added either before, during, or after the spoken lines, and participants move to the music.

Adaptation for the Hearing Impaired. The hearing impaired participant may be cued by a physical touch from a dance partner. The dance partner may hold hands with the handicapped participant and create the movement together.

The group poem may either be displayed in the room, or each participant may elect to hold a sign that displays his or her selected line.

With the introduction of these dance exercises, participants became more aware of the physical aspects of interpretation. They had, by this time, discovered that their bodies were still capable of movement. Those who were previously threatened by the aspects of learning dance steps, counting beats, and moving at the right time had their fears alleviated through the experience of freedom of movement. At one of the sites, however, two of the participants were accomplished dancers and, as a part of their oral history presentation, choreographed and performed a special dance number.

The wheelchair-bound participant's positive response was made audible through her laughter and joyous giggles as she waved her scarves and moved her chair to the sound of the music.

The integration of the visual arts was accomplished as a part of the various drama activities. The decorating of the group poem, and the construction of various properties for participatory theatre gave everyone the opportunity to become involved in a visual art experience. At one particular site, Oral History Booklets were compiled and each participant made a cover for his or her personal book.

Accommodations were made for the handicapped participants who required special help, through the assignment of a special helping partner.

VISUAL ARTS ACTIVITIES AS AN APPLIED THEATRE TECHNIQUE

The assignment of a helping partner not only aids the handicapped participant in feeling successful in the art activity, but aids the drama leader, as well. This method also helps to strengthen social contacts, which earlier may have been out of the question. With the aid of a helping partner, handicapped participants completed the following visual arts activities:

1. *Paperbag and paperplate masks for horses in* Canal Boats *and* Pumpkinseed, *the cat in* Emma. Supplies: grocery bags or plain paper plates, scraps of fabric, glue, colored construction paper, and scissors. Helping partners helped handicapped to design, cut, and glue faces onto grocery bags and paper plates. For the visually impaired, helping partner cut shapes and handed them to participant to feel. The shapes were then glued on to the bag or plate. The fabric shapes and heavy construction paper had enough texture and depth to enable blind participants to feel the final result.
2. *Paintings and pictures for* Emma. The visually impaired may again feel the texture of fabric and shapes of heavy construction paper to place and glue on to a background, thus creating a picture.
3. *Newspaper hats for* Caps for Sale. Supplies: Newspapers, tape. Helping partners helped handicapped to fold newspapers into the shape of sailors' hats. The blind participant was able to move his hands with his helper's assistance in folding and taping the hat. He felt the final product and was able to wear it!

The advantage of visual arts activities is that participants have a tangible product that they are proud of. They can see or, in the case of our blind participant, feel their creative efforts take shape and form. In drama, these visual arts products also become functional items because all are used as a part of the drama exercises or presentations. Participants also enjoyed giving their visual arts products to the children after the performances and projects had been completed. This gave the senior adults an even greater moment of pleasure as they experienced the opportunity to give a gift to someone they cared about.

One last technique used with the elderly participants was that of sociodrama. Although this method did not stand as an experience separate from the improvisational theatre exercises, the drama leader felt that they were worth mentioning because of their powerful effect upon two of the participants.

SOCIODRAMA AS AN APPLIED THEATRE TECHNIQUE

The term *sociodrama* is derived from the words *social* and *drama* and uses role-playing techniques as the vehicle for communication.

Basic improvisational theatre techniques are used, and the actors follow the Who, What, Where format. The focus of the scene, however, is some social problem a participant might be experiencing. Problems explored in a sociodrama may range from loneliness to misunderstandings with a family member. The "What," or conflict, of the scene is based upon an actual experience of the participant.

Some participants may elect to play themselves in the sociodrama improvisation, or they may elect to direct the scene and guide the action according to their perceptions of the problem. Others may prefer to sit and watch and gain insights through the actions of their peers.

The sociodrama scene may be stopped at any point, when an observer feels he or she has a possible solution to the problem. The scene may also be allowed to run its course, followed by a group discussion in which the observers make suggestions to the person experiencing the problem.

In one instance one of the participants, who was suffering from depression, asked that we build an improvisation around an incident that had happened to her 40 years ago. The incident involved her husband's desertion of the family and her subsequent increased responsibility of home, work, and family.

She elected to direct the scene as others acted out the roles of her husband, children, and employer. After the scene was over, other senior observers responded with, "You've always had a lot of things and people to take care of, haven't you?" The woman's response was, "Yes, I've never had the opportunity to just worry about me."

In working through this scene and watching the story unfold, the participant was able to gain added insight into her current feelings of depression, confusion, and anger with her children.

The information was shared with the site director, who, in turn, shared it with the proper medical personnel. Her attitude toward day-to-day tasks improved and she became very active in the drama group by suggesting projects, volunteering for extra work, and taking an active interest in preparing for final productions.

The effects of the drama program upon another depressed participant were stated by the site director: "We've never seen her smile before or talk so much to the other people here." In the case of this woman, who shied away from sociodrama and oral history theatre, involvement in the group was, for the time, sufficient evidence of her gradual social reintegration.

Working with handicapped elderly may either unveil "giftedness" in the arts or enhance their opportunities for acceptance within a group. It is important to strive for artistic integration, however, and to make the necessary adaptations of exercises to ensure their participation in every feasible way.

Thus, all four handicapped elderly participants were included in *all* projects and *all* exercises in some manner and were thought of *not* as handicapped but as contributing individuals. They developed friendships with their special helpers, and the helpers felt needed. The handicapped became respected members of the drama group through their total artistic participation.

REFERENCES

Anderson, W. "Pas de Psyche." *Human Behavior Magazine*, March 1977, 56-60.

Maker, J. 1977. *Providing Programs for the Gifted Handicapped*. Reston, Virginia: Council for Exceptional Children.

III

AN ASSESSMENT OF THE IMPACT OF APPLIED THEATRE TECHNIQUES ON THE ELDERLY

7

STUDY DESIGN AND METHODOLOGY

The study reported here employed a classical experimental design: comparing members of an experimental group, who participated in a weekly program of applied theatre for ten months, with members of a matched control group. The two groups were matched on important characteristics such as race, sex, age, income, health, and marital status. Members of the control group did not participate in the applied theatre experience. Those in the experimental and control groups were pretested (Time 1) and posttested (Time 2) on several important dependent variables. In this chapter we describe members of each group and how they were chosen and discuss measurement techniques for each of the major dependent variables.

SUBJECTS

To test the impact of participation in applied theatre, 106 elderly people at seven nutrition sites in Richmond and northern Virginia were selected to participate in weekly sessions led by a trained drama expert for ten months. Participants from each site who volunteered to be a part of the program composed the experimental group. A matched control group of 27, chosen from another nutrition site in Richmond, was used for comparison. Random assignment of participants to experimental and control groups was impossible due to the shortage of numbers of able and willing volunteers. Not everyone desires to try something new and to be "studied."

Participants were chosen by contacting the directors of nutrition sites in Richmond and northern Virginia. Seven nutrition centers were chosen for the final study, two in Richmond and five in Alexandria and Arlington. At the five sites in northern Virginia, the theatre sessions were conducted by a qualified and experienced expert in theatre arts and senior theatre. Trained volunteers, who were members of the staff, conducted the sessions at the two Richmond sites. Theatre groups ranged in size from five to 25 members. The matched controls were chosen from another Richmond center. It was not possible to obtain a control group from the centers in northern Virginia; however, the controls chosen from Richmond were like the participants in northern Virginia in most major respects.

All participants (controls and experimentals) were over 55 and 90 percent were over 60. Ninety percent of the participants (controls and experimentals) were formerly employed as blue-collar workers, particularly in manual labor, factory work, domestic and restaurant work, and office or clerical work, and most had a high school education or less. Table 6 shows that members of the control group and experimental group are fairly well matched on sex, race, and marital status, variables identified in the literature as related to life satisfaction. Participants were predominantly black, female, and unmarried. Members of the control and experimental groups were also from the same socioeconomic class and neighborhoods. All were in good or fair health.

TABLE 6. Demographic Characteristics of Study Participants

Group	Male	Female	Black	White	Married	Unmarried
Experimental	29%	71%	85%	15%	29%	71%
Control	27%	73%	100%	0%	17%	83%

Each experimental group at each of the seven nutrition sites studied was unique. Groups differed in size, characteristics of members, and in the way in which the dramatic experience was participated in. The smallest group had only five members; the largest had 25. Due to the small numbers in each group, any percentage distribution of characteristics must be interpreted with caution. With this in mind, a site-specific breakdown of demographic characteristics of group members is presented in Table 7.

TABLE 7. Demographic Characteristics of Study Participants at Each Site

Site	Male	Female	Black	White	Married	Unmarried
A (N=11)	18%	82%	82%	18%	27%	73%
B (N=10)	0%	100%	0%	100%	0%	100%
C (N=5)	40%	60%	0%	100%	40%	60%
D (N=21)	29%	71%	62%	38%	10%	90%
E (N=13)	8%	92%	46%	54%	15%	85%
F (N=25)	12%	88%	100%	0%	8%	92%
G (N=21)	29%	71%	95%	5%	29%	71%

Differential implementation of the drama program at each site has already been described in detail in Chapter 3.

DEPENDENT VARIABLES

Participants and nonparticipants were pretested and posttested using a global question on life satisfaction, as well as by questions assessing perceptions of health, loneliness, and subjective age identification.

To assess life satisfaction, subjects were asked to respond to the question, Overall, how satisfied are you with your life? The response choices were Satisfied and Not Satisfied. Global self-report measures of life satisfaction, such as the one used in this study, have been used quite frequently, particularly when large scale secondary data sources have been analyzed (Rose, 1955; Streib, 1956; Cantril, 1965; Davis, 1974; Lebo, 1953).

Wilson (1967) suggests that the "advantages of a simple self-rating over many adjustment measures would seem to be that it will (a) include less irrelevant factorial complexity, (b) be easier to obtain, and (c) have at least face validity as a measure of avowed happiness." This measure of life satisfaction is a subjective form of social indicator because it is based on self-reports of the individual's personal life experience. It can be argued that subjective measures yield objective information in the sense of registering perceptions and emotional states (Andrews and Withey, 1973).

Several researchers have found that self-reports of psychological well-being have considerable reliability and validity (Bradburn, 1969; Robinson and Shaver, 1969; Lohmann, 1977).

To measure loneliness respondents were asked, How often do you feel lonely? Response choices included: Most of the Time, Much of the Time, Some of the Time, Hardly Ever, and Never. Such a global, undimensional approach to measuring loneliness has been extensively used in the past (Bradburn, 1969; Maisel, 1969; Lowenthal, Thurner, and Chiriboga, 1975; Atchley, 1976; Shanas et al., 1968; Berg et al., 1981; Huyck and Hoyer, 1982; Kivett, 1979). The reliability of these measures has not been reported, but self-rating measures, such as the one employed in this study and the others referred to, obviously have content or face validity.

Subjective age identification was assessed by asking respondents, How do you see yourself as far as age goes? Response choices included Old, Middle-Aged, and Young. How one views one's self in terms of age is one important component of self-concept. Self-identification as old generally carries negative connotations (Blau, 1963; Kogan and Wallach, 1961; Deutsch and Solomon, 1959; Youmans, 1968; Bennett and Eckman, 1973). The method used in this study to assess subjective age identification has been used in earlier studies by Blau (1956) and Hoyt et al. (1980).

REFERENCES

Andrews, F. M., and S. Withey. 1973. *Developing Measures of Perceived Life Quality: Results From Several National Surveys.* Ann Arbor, Michigan: University of Michigan Institute for Social Research.

Atchley, R. C. 1976. "Selected Social and Psychological Differences Between Men and Women in Later Life." *Journal of Gerontology* 31:204-211.

Bennett, R., and J. Eckman. 1973. "Attitudes Toward Aging: A Critical Examination of Recent Literature and Implications for Future Research." In *The Psychology of Adult Development,* edited by C. Eisdorfer and M. P. Lawton, pp. 575-597. Washington, D.C.: American Psychological Association.

Berg, S., D. Mellstrom, G. Persson, and A. Svanborg. 1981. "Loneliness in the Swedish Aged." *Journal of Gerontology* 36:342-349.

Blau, Z. 1963. "Changes in Status and Age Identification." In *Gerontology--A Book of Readings*, edited by C. Vedder, pp. 78-87. Springfield, Illinois: Charles C. Thomas.

Bradburn, N. 1969. *The Structure of Psychological Well-Being*. Chicago: Aldine.

Cantril, H. 1965. *The Patterns of Human Concerns*. New Brunswick, New Jersey: Rutgers University Press.

Davis, J. A. 1974. *National Data Program for the Social Sciences*. Chicago: National Opinion Research Center.

Deutsch, M., and L. Solomon. 1959. "Reactions to Evaluations by Others as Influenced by Self Evaluations." *Sociometry* 22:93-112.

Hoyt, D. R., M. A. Kaiser, G. R. Peters, and N. Babchuk. 1980. "Life Satisfaction and Activity Theory: A Multidimensional Approach." *Journal of Gerontology* 33:935-941.

Huyck, M. H., and W. J. Hoyer. 1982. *Adult Development and Aging*. Belmont, California: Wadsworth.

Kivett, V. R. 1979. "Discriminators of Loneliness Among the Rural Elderly: Implications for Intervention." *The Gerontologist* 19:108-115.

Kogan, N., and M. A. Wallach. 1961. "Age Changes in Attitudes and Values." *Journal of Gerontology* 16:272-279.

Kuhlen, R. G. 1948. "Age Trends in Adjustment During the Adult Years as Reflected in Happiness Ratings." *American Journal of Psychology* 3:307.

Lebo, D. 1953. "Some Factors Said to Make for Happiness in Old Age." *Journal of Clinical Psychology* 9:385-390.

Lohmann, N. 1977. "Correlates of Life Satisfaction, Morale and Adjustment Measures." *Journal of Gerontology* 32:73-75.

Lowenthal, M. F., M. Thurner, and D. Chiriboga. 1975. *Four Stages of Life*. San Francisco: Jossey-Bass.

Maisel, R. 1969. *Report of the Continuing Audit of Public Attitudes and Concerns*. Boston: Harvard Medical School Laboratory of Community Psychiatry.

Robinson, J. P., and M. Shaver. 1969. *Measures of Social Psychological Attitudes*. Ann Arbor, Michigan: University of Michigan Survey Research Center.

Rose, A. M. 1955. "Factors Associated with the Life Satisfaction of Middle Class, Middle Aged Persons." *Marriage and Family Living* 17:15-19.

Shanas, E., P. Townsend, D. Wedderburn, H. Friis, P. Milhoj, and J. Stenhouwer. 1968. *Old People in Three Industrial Societies*. New York: Atherton.

Streib, G. 1956. "Morale of the Retired." *Social Problems* 3:270-276.

Wilson, W. 1967. "Correlates of Avowed Happiness." *Psychological Bulletin* 67:294-306.

Youmans, E. C. 1968. "Orientations of Old Age." *The Gerontologist* 8:153-158.

8

DATA ANALYSIS AND FINDINGS

Pretest and posttest data were computer analyzed using analysis of change scores (Campbell and Stanley, 1963), to determine whether or not members of the experimental group changed significantly more on the three measures than did members of the control group after participation in the ten-month program of applied theatre. To calculate change scores, we subtracted the mean score at Time 1 from the mean score at Time 2 for experimental and control groups and calculated the change in means for each group. A one-tailed test of differences in changed means was then applied to test for statistical significance of change from Time 1 to Time 2. As Campbell and Stanley (1963) note in their book, "The most widely used acceptable test is to compute for each group pretest-posttest gain scores and to compute a t between experimental and control groups on these gain scores. . . ." (p. 23). Separate analyses were run for men and women, married and unmarried.

Qualitative analyses of excerpts from diaries kept by the drama leader and participants, interviews with participants, systematically recorded observations of group sessions, review of anecdotes, and consideration of case studies were also performed.

QUANTITATIVE RESULTS

The quantitative analyses of change scores revealed some significant changes in major dependent variables. When compared to the control group, those in the experimental group improved considerably on questions of life satisfaction, loneliness, and subjective age identification from Time 1 to Time 2. Participants in the applied theatre program after ten months were happier and more satisfied with life in general and perceived themselves as less lonely and younger than members of the control group, who did not participate. When all experimentals were compared with controls, the change in subjective age identification from T_1 to T_2 was not statistically significant. When the analysis was conducted comparing only those participants who were from the five sites in northern Virginia working with the experienced drama expert with the controls, however, the difference from T_1 to T_2 was statistically significant. Table 10 reports the results of this analysis. Tables 8, 9, and 10 display results of the quantitative analyses.

TABLE 8. Mean Scores on Global Measure of Life Satisfaction

Group	Time 1	Time 2	Change
Experimental	.84	.97	+.13
Control	.87	.92	+.05
	$t(106) = 1.85, P = < .03$		

TABLE 9. Mean Scores on Loneliness

Group	Time 1	Time 2	Change
Experimental	2.7	2.3	−.4
Control	2.5	2.4	−.1
	$t(135) = 1.91, P = < .03$		

TABLE 10. Mean Scores on Subjective Age Identification

Group	Time 1	Time 2	Change
Experimental	1.9	2.1	+0.2
Control	1.9	1.9	+0.0
	$t(54) = 2.83, P = < .01$		

A glance at the tables reveals that scores on loneliness and global life satisfaction for members of the experimental and control groups are different at Time 1. A test of differences between the means at Time 1 revealed that these differences were not satisfactorily significant (life satisfaction $t(106) = 0.62$; loneliness $t(135) = 0.75$).

The gerontological literature reporting on variables related to life satisfaction of the elderly is extensive. There is general agreement that certain variables such as health, economic situation, gender, and marital status influence life satisfaction in late life (Adams, 1971; Knapp, 1976; Palmore and Kivett, 1977; Palmore and Luikart, 1972; Sauer, 1977; Spreitzer and Snyder, 1974; Wolk and Telleen, 1976; Markides and Martin, 1979). In this study there was very little variance on financial situation or on health as measured by responses to the question, How would you describe your health at present (Excellent, Good, Fair, Poor)? All subjects were from lower income backgrounds, and over 80 percent described their health as good or fair. These two important variables, identified in the literature as significantly affecting life satisfaction of the elderly, were, thus, automatically controlled for in the present study. To assure that findings were not the result of differences in gender or marital status, separate analyses were run for men and women, married and unmarried. The results in Tables 8, 9, and 10 were essentially the same for men and women, married and not married.

QUALITATIVE RESULTS

Qualitative analyses of diary excerpts, recorded observations of the group leader, and interviews with participants lent support to the quantitative results just presented. Qualitative analyses revealed that elderly black participants in the applied theatre program had their lives changed. Participants became more and more comfortable with each other as a group as the sessions continued. They opened up and expressed feelings. They learned to cooperate and work together as a group. Individuals laughed a lot and gained enough self-confidence to perform in front of others. Some with psychiatric problems opened up and came out of their withdrawn states during the course of the project. Many noted on their own, either through written or oral comments, an improvement in their outlook on life, in themselves and how they felt physically or mentally, in their personal lives, and in their relations with family and friends.

The following excerpts from the leaders' diaries are illustrative of some of the positive changes that occurred as a result of this ten-month experience for seniors.

> One participant confined to a wheelchair who had danced as a youth participated as a handicapped dancer and was overjoyed by the experience.

> One other participant was under psychiatric care for extreme depression when she joined the drama group. After participating in the group, she told us that her participation in the oral history theatre let her understand some of the past events in her life and put them in perspective. In the course of ten months this participant blossomed as she became more expressive, less withdrawn, and happier.

> Another woman in one of the other groups was also severely depressed and confused when she joined the drama sessions. Before participating in the drama group this resident had been ignored by fellow members at the site. When she started participating in the creative drama group, members of the group took an active interest in her, helping her with her script work and memorization. As a result of the attention, this woman became more sociable and responded openly, verbally and physically, to others, something she had not previously done.

> Most participants at the various sites had not interacted with each other as individuals before the drama group was formed, according to site directors. An interesting phenomenon occurred at the sites after the groups formed.

Members of the groups became friends and they interacted with each other on a regular basis at the centers outside the drama groups. They became much more active and sociable as a result of their participation in the drama groups.

All of the sites were isolated from intergenerational contact when the study began. The introduction of children into the sites had a very positive effect on elderly participants. They became much more physically and verbally expressive, more animated (smiling, laughing, touching) and happier and more enthusiastic.

The following quotations from participants are illustrative of the ways in which many of the seniors perceived the impact of participation in drama on their lives: "It gives me a little pleasure out of life," said a septuagenarian at one site; "I think it's kept me on my toes and interested," said one 77-year-old participant who credited his experience in creative dramatics as responsible for his recovery from a recent heart attack; and "It has carried me back into the world again," said one aged participant.

REFERENCES

Adams, D. L. 1971. "Correlates of Satisfaction Among the Aged." *The Gerontologist* 11:64-108.

Campbell, D. T., and J. C. Stanley. 1963. "Experimental and Quasi-experimental Designs for Research." In *Handbook of Research and Teaching*, edited by N. L. Gage. Chicago: Rand McNally.

Knapp, M. 1976. "Predicting the Dimensions of Life Satisfaction." *Journal of Gerontology* 31:595-604.

Markides, K. and H. Martin. 1979. "A Causal Model of Life Satisfaction Among the Elderly." *Journal of Gerontology* 34:86-93.

Palmore, E., and V. Kivett. 1977. "Changes in Life Satisfaction: A Longitudinal Study of Persons Aged 46-70." *Journal of Gerontology* 32:311-316.

Palmore, E., and C. Luikart. 1972. "Health and Social Factors Related to Life Satisfaction." *Journal of Health and Social Behavior* 13:68-80.

Sauer, M. 1977. "Morale of the Urban Aged: A Regression Analysis by Race." *Journal of Gerontology* 32:600-608.

Spreitzer, E. and E. Snyder. 1974. "Correlates of Life Satisfaction Among the Aged." *Journal of Gerontology* 29:454-458.

Wolk, S., and S. Telleen. 1976. "Psychological and Social Correlates of Life Satisfaction As a Function of Residential Constraint." *Journal of Gerontology* 31:89-98.

9

CONCLUSIONS AND SUGGESTIONS FOR FUTURE RESEARCH

The study reported here employed a classical experimental design, comparing members of an experimental group (103 elderly, 95 percent of whom were black, chosen from seven nutrition sites in northern Virginia and Richmond to participate in weekly creative drama sessions for ten months) and matched control group (27 black elderly chosen from another study site in Richmond, Virginia, and matched for race, sex, age, and marital status) at Time 1 (pretest) and Time 2 (posttest) on several important variables. Analysis of change scores from Time 1 to Time 2 on life satisfaction, self-perceived loneliness, and subjective age identification revealed that after ten months of applied theatre, elderly participants were significantly happier and less lonely than those who did not participate (controls). Participants at the five sites in northern Virginia, who were led by a trained, experienced drama leader, also identified themselves as younger than members of the control group after ten months of participation in the applied theatre program. All results were significant at or below the .05 level of probability. Qualitative analysis of recorded observations, diary excerpts of drama leaders and participants, and interviews with participants revealed that those who took part in the creative drama program opened up and expressed feelings, became close as a group, and made friendships that were carried out of the drama sessions. They also experienced joy and excitement and in general became happier, better functioning human beings.

The study is the first systematic, controlled investigation of the effects of participation in a program of applied theatre on seniors and on black seniors in particular. The results are encouraging and indicate that applied theatre techniques offer one avenue of recreational activity that black elderly people can participate in effectively, can enjoy, and can benefit from greatly. It is a form of art therapy that gets them involved in new and meaningful social roles and activities, socializing with others in a friendly environment, and that allows for creative expression of feelings, release of tension, and exploration of issues that are significant to the elderly, such as the issue of death. Participating in applied theatre provides a success experience for elderly individuals in which they can achieve a degree of self-mastery, control over their environment, and feelings of competence and accomplishment of goals.

This study would seem to suggest that more programs using the creative arts, such as dance, music, and drama, should be implemented for the elderly. This study was a pilot study, a first attempt to assess the effects of one form of creative recreational therapy on elderly persons. Certainly, more studies need to be done identifying other variables that are important to look at, that are better techniques of measurement, and, in particular, that specify those particular techniques of applied theatre that are most effective with different types of seniors (black and white, institutionalized and community, etc.).

THEORETICAL IMPLICATIONS AND DIRECTIONS FOR FUTURE RESEARCH

Results of the impact of participation in applied theatre that have been reported from both quantitative and qualitative analyses reveal that those elderly individuals who took part in such a program became happier and felt less lonely. They saw themselves as younger. Participants opened up and expressed feelings, became close as a group, and made firm friendships. These results lend additional support to the well-known activity theory of aging, which suggests that those elderly individuals who remain active and engaged in roles and groups are happier and age more successfully than those who disengage from activity in their later years.

This disengagement theory, on the other hand, received little support. Members of the experimental group were anything but disengaged. They not only increased their level of recreational activity each week through active participation in the program but also expanded their contacts and friendships outside of the program, increasing their level of social activity in general. At some sites, members of the group organized and put on plays and shows for other residents of the center. These performances required a high level of activity above and beyond the weekly sessions. They were big projects, and elderly participants were very busy and fully engaged in them. The performances were a huge success with other members of the nutrition sites and their families; the senior artists were proud of themselves and their performance and felt good about themselves.

Nutrition sites are age segregated environments; and the applied theatre groups were composed of only older members. Members shared a common past, present, and future. They had all experienced the same historical and social events and had similar values, needs, and concerns. They were all at the same life stage, having raised their children, retired from their jobs, and experiencing financial and health problems. The issues of death and dying had major importance for all of them at this stage in their lives. This common ground helped members of the group relate to each other and share easily with one another and allowed for similar responses to particular music, activities, and exercises. For example, enacting a scene with canal boats or telling a story of an early romance elicited similar feelings, memories, and responses in members and made for easy discussion.

The social integration theory of aging suggests that elderly individuals who live among their age peers will be better adjusted and happier than those who live in mixed aged settings, because age peers provide a basis of social integration and social bonding. This study supports the social integration theory. Interacting in small groups with age peers on a weekly basis was a very positive experience for the elderly participants in our study. The similarity in age and common backgrounds, history, values, needs, concerns and problems, which stem from the age similarity, enhanced the applied theatre experience for participants. It is impossible to scientifically speculate on what kinds of results would have been obtained if the groups under study were mixed age groups, because we had no such groups in the study. However, based on interviews, observation, and diary analyses, we feel that the applied theatre experience would not have had the same dramatic impact on elderly participants if they had not participated in groups with age peers. Future studies of mixed aged groups could shed more light on this question and provide a further test of the social integration theory.

Future studies could also look at such questions as which applied theatre techniques are most easily implemented in community settings? Which techniques are most successful with nursing home residents? What are the effects of participation in applied theatre for elderly members of mixed aged groups? What combination of art, drama, music, and dance is the most effective with elderly residents of nursing homes? What combination is most effective for the elderly living in the community? These and other questions for future investigation abound. It is hoped that the results of the study reported in this book will encourage others to examine these and other questions in more sophisticated ways. Such a research agenda must be addressed if we are to adequately meet the needs of the many different types of elderly individuals in a wide range of settings.

THE ROLE OF THE ARTIST IN THE SPECIFIC EXPERIMENTAL DESIGN

The role of the artist in a specific experimental design must be defined in relation to the scientist. For the role of an artist involved in a project of this nature is quite different from the role of an artist as artist. The sacred union between scientist and artist has drastically changed since the Renaissance, during which the fusion between art and science was at its height.

The work "renaissance" itself is indicative of the unusual cultural attitude of the time during which one of the most important discoveries was perspective. Not only did artists recognize the power of perspective but so did inventors, architects, and scientists. They found themselves in a natural union, seeking advice and opinions when needed and seeking each other's approval upon the completion of ideas.

The union between the artist and scientist today seems accidental. Major universities suffer the loss of unknown discoveries as a result of segregation of departments. Only recently, one major university, respected for its gerontological research and nationally known for its center on aging, stated that its resources and research in the field of arts and the aging were very limited. Yet, the information provided for us, and stated briefly in this book, attests to the fact that elderly artists continue to contribute to the world, without hesitation or regard to age, but rather with a powerful insight and respect for life. Might we, then, look into the aging process of the artist and gain a different perspective?

In this study we attempted to unite the fields of theatre art and science to gain some new perspective concerning success in the aging process. And if we are to see important discoveries within this century, then three necessary steps must be taken to unite the scientific and aesthetic talents of man. The initial step begins with a commitment to interaction.

COMMITMENT TO INTERACTION--ART/SCIENCE

Interaction begins with the artist's and scientist's need for a new perspective. It may begin as a solitary need, which does not even extend beyond one's own field. If, however, a commitment is made to the discovery of a new perspective, both parties may seek original avenues of exploration. These new avenues may lead two seemingly unrelated fields to an expressed intent of unified discovery.

The role of the artist expands through his or her commitment to the scientist, for it is through this commitment that the artist accepts a position that compromises pure art and complements scientific discovery. As the theatre artist becomes involved in the process of art and aesthetic development with senior participants, there exists a certain necessary detachment vital to the observation and measurement process. This is not to say that this detachment is not present in the training of professional artists. For a professional arts trainer must maintain a certain distance for the evaluation of the student artist's works and subsequent needs. But there is a limiting force when dealing with numerical measurement that requires the artist to compromise and complement.

If artist and scientist can successfully master this stage, the second phase of unified discovery leads to shared observation and interaction between the artist and the scientist.

INTERACTION AND SHARED OBSERVATION--ART/SCIENCE

The role of the artist in observation becomes two-fold as the focus is divided between artistic considerations and measurable objectives.

The union with the scientist may, at this point, be very close, as both communicate often and share their expertise in field-related observations. The relationship may also become segregated at this point, with the artist making observations and the scientist tabulating designated measurements throughout the project.

It is at this point that the role of the artist becomes difficult, for it is an artistic hardship to forfeit aesthetic development and gather measurable documentation. The elderly participants, although cooperative, become frustrated with forms and questionnaires and the artist's role becomes one of explaining the importance of the documentation and providing additional outlets for expression. For example, one participant became very frustrated with the questionnaires and stated that he did not feel his answers on the form completely described the changes he had made while involved in the applied theatre project. The participant was given the opportunity to record his feelings in narrative form and, as a result, felt more positive about participating in the study and less hesitant about documentation.

In our study, then, we found that the combination of qualitative and quantitative data to be the most successful approach in developing our new unified perspective. Upon completion of documentation through questionnaires, journal entries, and actual participation, the role of the artist and scientist in relation to the project progresses to that of evaluator.

EVALUATION--ART/SCIENCE

The artist, as evaluator, must develop three separate perspectives in evaluating the applied theatre project with senior adults. The first perspective focuses on the individual as an artist and his or her subsequent aesthetic development. The second perspective concentrates on the progression of the group as an artistic company. The final perspective concerns the data collected, reviewed, and summarized by the scientist.

The artist, in evaluating this information, becomes, once again, the investigator, in trying to evaluate the relationship and impact of the empirical data upon the artistic growth of the participants. The reaction to art is easy to measure. It is the process of art itself that is so difficult to provide accountability for. The artist, then, is dependent upon the scientist for the design of appropriate measurements to assess the process of art.

Jonas Salk (1973) strongly supports the efforts of integrated fields of knowledge in saying:

> Man possesses foresight and a capacity to imagine and relate seemingly unconnected events. Although artists, poets,

and those engaged in "creative" work are thought to be especially endowed with those qualities, many others also have such attributes. If more individuals become sufficiently involved in this respect, they will be capable of further development so as to be more sensitively responsive individually and to each other, resulting in increased empathy and augmenting "coalescence" (p. 55).

It was, then, through the combined efforts of the scientist and the artist in this study that we not only found applied theatre to have a positive impact upon the process of aging, but we also discovered a new perspective concerning the union of measurement and design between art and science. For this project and for future projects of this nature, this means advancement in applied theatre techniques and, consequently, greater fulfillment in the process of aging.

REFERENCES

Salk, J. 1973. *The Survival of the Wisest.* New York: Harper & Row.

APPENDIX

APPENDIX

COMPOSITION OF THE DAY
(Drama, Playwriting)

Players: Full group
Objective: Participants will become familiar with use of visual still life as a stimulus for playwriting and improvisational theatre techniques
Supplies: Prop box filled with objects brought from home such as, items from the kitchen, garage, bedroom, clothing items no longer in use, string, empty cans, papers, pencils, etc.

1. One participant is designated to select items from the prop box and arrange them as a still life composition in a designated area of the room.
2. Participants close their eyes while still life is being arranged.
3. Participants open eyes when still life has been completed and fill in the following information on paper:
If this were the opening of the play, how would you complete the following information:
Who:
What:
Where:
First line in the play:
Ending line:

ORIGINAL SCRIPTS--*SPLICES OF LIFE*

Splice of Life #1--GOOD TIMES IN THE CITY
Setting: An office in a building in New York
Characters: Narrator
Photographer--Millie
Acrobat
Party Hostess
Party Guests
Maid

NARRATOR

(*Sign is placed on easel for audience to see that says, "Good Times in the City"*)

(*Appears down-stage left.*) This is a splice of life that has probably happened to only one person in a million.

Let's go back to the year 1962. (*Lights come up onstage to reveal an office decorated for a celebration. There is a long table center stage and chairs are scattered about the room.*) Millie has just gone to New York to work as a photographer. She was greeted warmly and even given a reception. (*Other actors begin filing in. Millie and a guest are center stage. As actors come in they cross to Millie and shake her hand and then disperse to various areas onstage.*) She met many wonderful people there. (*The acrobat enters down-stage left and crosses to center-stage left.*) But there was one man in particular who caught her eye. (*Waltz begins to play. Millie turns and catches the eye of the acrobat. He goes to her and leads her downstage, and they begin to dance. The maid has a difficult time weaving in and out of the guests and she and the dancers narrowly escape a collision.*)

As the dance ended, dinner was announced. (*Maid indicates to party hostess that the dinner is ready.*)

PARTY HOSTESS

Alright, everyone, dinner is ready. But first let's have a toast. . . . To Millie! (*All guests raise their glasses and freeze in position.*)

NARRATOR

Millie turned to her magnificent dance partner and said,

MILLIE

Let's go get something to eat!

ACROBAT

Well, ah. . . . I'm really not . . .

MILLIE

Come on! Aren't you hungry?

ACROBAT

Well, to tell you the truth . . .

MILLIE

Come on! Let's get something to eat! (*Millie leads him to table.*)

ACROBAT

I can't! I'm not even supposed to be here!

MILLIE

(*Stops in her tracks.*) Are you trying to tell me you weren't invited to this party?

ACROBAT

That's right.

MILLIE
I'm sorry, but I don't think I quite understand.
ACROBAT
Well, you see, I don't really work for this company. I just happened to be in the building when I heard all this commotion and I thought I'd stop in.
MILLIE
Well, where did you come from!?
ACROBAT
Well, actually, I'm the star trapeze artist for the Barnum & Bailey Circus.
MAID
You're what?! (*Other actors release their freeze and react with ad-libs of "What?" "What did he say?" "He's a what?"*)
NARRATOR
(*Steps down-stage left.*) As I said before, this is a splice of life that could only happen to one in a million--dancing the night away in New York City with a trapeze artist! (*Actors begin to hum "Put Your Arms Around Me Honey" and Millie and trapeze artist exit down-stage right with their arms around each other.*)

Actors begin to sing: Put your arms around me, honey,
Hold me tight.
Huddle up and cuddle up
With all your might.
Oh, oh, won't you roll
Those eyes,
Eyes that I just idolize
When you look at me
My heart begins to float
Then it starts a rockin'
Like a motor boat.
Oh, oh, I never knew
any girl like you.

(*As they quietly change the set to a buggy--chairs are arranged to accommodate couples sitting in a buggy--and the Narrator now becomes the "horse." Tablecloths are changed to gingham covers and the upstage and down-stage left areas now resemble the inside of a barn where there is a dance. The actors change formal scarves to country hats and ties and Narrator # 2 takes her position down-stage left.*)

Splice of Life #2--GOOD TIMES IN THE COUNTRY
NARRATOR
(*Sign is placed on an easel for audience to see that says, "Good Times in the Country"*) Now, what you just saw was a splice of life about the city. But what about the country? What about courtships and riding in a wagon to a party? (*Actors in wagon and the "horse" sing "Put Your Arms Around Me Honey."*)
ROY
Whoa!!!! (*Horse gives Roy a dirty look.*)
NARRATOR
When you got to the country dance you might pull some taffy first . . . (*Actors are laughing and talking excitedly as they get out of the imaginary wagon and greet others at the party. There are four cardplayers located stage left. Actors from the wagon cross up-stage and get "taffy"--old pantyhose--and begin to twist it and laugh.*)

And, of course, there was always a game of cards or checkers! (*Actors cross over to the cardplayers and ad-lib, "Cone on, pull some taffy with us!" "Can you help me with this?" "Yuck!" The cardplayers become entangled in the taffy. Square dancing music starts to fade in.*)

And what would a country dance be without a polka! (*Roy and Millie cross center stage and dance a polka. Other actors gather around in a semicircle and clap in time to the music.*)
And at the end of the evening, we'd all pile back in the wagon! (*Entire cast, including the Narrator and the cardplayers, pile back into the wagon, which is now very crowded.*)
ROY
Didn't even have to steer, 'cause the horses knew the way home. GIDDYUP! (*"Horse" makes the motion of moving and entire cast sings "Shine on Harvest Moon." The cast repeats the song and goes out into the audience and encourages them to join in the song. Cast comes back to center stage for a bow at the end of the song.*)
THE END

ORIGINAL SCRIPTS--*LUNCH AT THE WHITE HOUSE*
Setting: The formal dining room of the White House
Characters: Madame Bon-Bon
                Senator Apple (representing New York)
                Henry Kissing-her
                Jackie Oasis
                Queen Liz
                Prince Phil

Two community representatives
The maid
The president

(As the curtain opens, a maid bustles around the table in preparation for the dignitaries who are soon to arrive. She knocks over a glass and looks around to see if anyone has noticed. The President enters. The Maid nervously curtsies.)

PRESIDENT

Good afternoon.

MAID

Good afternoon, sir.

PRESIDENT

The guests should soon be arriving. Is everything ready?

MAID

Oh, yes, sir.

PRESIDENT

Good. *(He takes his place at the center of the seating arrangement. "Pomp and Circumstance" begins to slowly fade in. The President stands. The dignitaries line up and as the maid introduces each one of them, the President shakes their hands and gestures toward the table for them to find their place. All guests remain standing until the President sits.)*

MAID

Announcing the arrival of Madam Bon-Bon. *(Madam Bon-Bon floats in spouting something that sounds like French.)*

Announcing the arrival of Senator Apple. *(Senator Apple holds up a large "Big Apple" poster for the audience to see.)*

SENATOR APPLE

I love New York! Don't you?

MAID

Announcing the arrival of Henry Kissing-her. *(He says nothing, but does smile at the audience.)*

Announcing the arrival of Jackie Oasis.

JACKIE OASIS

Ohhhhhhhh. I just *love* parties. *(Looks around the room.)* How tacky.

MAID

Announcing the arrival of Queen Liz and Prince Phil.

PRINCE PHIL

Where's the food?

QUEEN LIZ

Behave yourself!

MAID

Announcing the arrival of . . . (*She whispers to the remaining two guests.*) Excuse me, but who are you?

COMMUNITY REPRESENTATIVE

We're community representatives, and we're here to do a survey!

PRESIDENT

Please be seated everyone. (*Everyone does so.*) I'm delighted that you could attend this special White House Luncheon. I think you'll find the food quite good. We're having . . . uh, (*He turns to the maid.*) What are we having?

MAID

Cheese, sir.

PRESIDENT

Ah, yes, of course. Cheese. (*The guests make faces. The Maid begins to serve what seems like a seven course meal, all variations on the theme of cheese.*)

ONE COMMUNITY REPRESENTATIVE

Mr. President, it must be wonderful living in the White House all the time.

PRESIDENT

Well, we do find it quite comfortable.

JACKIE OASIS

Would you just look at this china? Where did they get china like this?

SENATOR APPLE

Mr. President, what would you most like to be remembered for?

MADAM BON-BON

(*Under her breath.*) His cheese!

PRESIDENT

Well, I'd like to be remembered for my fairness and . . .

PRINCE PHIL

Ahhhh . . . (*Begins to choke on his cheese.*)

QUEEN LIZ

I told you not to stuff your face!

HENRY KISSING-HER

Mr. President, what is this we're eating now?

PRESIDENT

Oh, this, why it's . . . (*He turns to the Maid.*) What *is* this we're eating now?

MAID

"Roast of cheese," sir.

PRESIDENT

Why, of course. "Roast of cheese." (*The guests begin to look like they have upset stomachs.*)

APPENDIX / 191

JACKIE OASIS
Would you look at this china!
MAID
Shall I serve dessert, sir?
PRESIDENT
By all means! Wait a minute . . . What *is* for dessert?
MAID
Why, cheese flavored ice-cream, sir!
PRINCE PHIL
Well, the Queen and I've gotta be running now, Mr. President.
PRESIDENT
Oh, so soon? But, I didn't get to ask you about your trip over . . . (*As the President is talking, Prince Phil gets up to leave and drags the Queen with him. Others follow suit, making excuses as they leave. The President is left alone at the table.*)
MAID
(*She slowly approaches him after having witnessed the hasty exit of all guests.*) Shall I serve dessert, sir?
PRESIDENT
By all means, please *don't*. (*The President exits as the Maid stares with dismay at the leftover cheese dishes.*)
THE END

The President Speaks

SUGGESTIONS FOR MUSIC

o "Beethoven Piano Concerto No. 3 in C minor," Adolph Drescher, Piano Royal Danish Symphony Orchestra. George Richter, Conductor. CMS Records, 14 Warren Street, N.Y., N.Y. 10007

o "Dance-A-Long," music composed by B. J. Walberg. Material edited by Marjorie Mazia, Folkway Records, 701 7th Avenue, N.Y, N.Y. 10011

o "The Piatnitsky Folk Chorus and Orchestra," Monitor Records, 156 Fifth Avenue, N.Y., N.Y. 10011

o "Sebastian" by Gian Carlo Menotti. London Symphony Orchestra. Jose Serebrier, Conductor. CMS/Desoto Records, 14 Warren Street, N.Y., N.Y. 10007

INDEX

Abkhasians, 24; role of elderly, 24
Acting Up!: An Innovative Approach to Creative Drama for Older Adults, 66
activity theory, 11, 25-27, 176
actor and real-life characters, relationship between, 115
actor training techniques, 106
actors and stresses, age and creativity, 54
Actor's Theatre of Louisville, 80, 116
adult behavior, age effects and generation-related differences, 42-43
advertising, role playing for, 84
aesthetic environment, establishing, 101
age, 12, 14; chronological, changes in, 12; creative growth, 14; and creativity, 36-47; and productivity, 36-47
Age and Achievement, 36
age-concentrated environments, 31
aged, *see* elderly
aged subculture, development of, 31
"ageism," 8, 9
age peers, 29; as basis of social integration, 177; living among, 31; meeting with, 32; social gains for those living among, 30
age-segregated communities, 29; qualitative studies of, 30
aging, 5-11; activity theory of, 176; cross-societal theory of, 8; factors affecting, 46; functionalism and, 23; Greek playwright's image of, 70-73; modern playwright's images of, 77; negative aspects of, 74; peak periods of creativity and, 37; problems of, 5-10; restoration playwright's image of, 75-77; Shakespeare's image of, 73-75; social integration theory of, 177; social theories of, 21-32; successful adaptation to, 10-11
Alliance for Arts Education of the American Theatre Association Senior Adult Theatre Project, 15
Amber Area Arts Alliance of Amber, Pennsylvania, 13
American Theatre Association, 13, 80
"anomic," 7
anxiety, 7
applied theatre, 12-15, 65-68; benefits, 14; first controlled, scientific investigation of, 16-17; growing interest in, 14; minority elderly and, 15

applied theatre techniques, assessment of impact of, 163-180
Aristophanes, 70, 72
artist: as evaluator, 180; role of in observation, 179; role of in specific experimental design, 178-79
artists and architects, age and creativity, 53-54
art/science: commitment to interaction, 179; evaluation, 180; interaction and shared observation, 179
autodidactic, 48, 52

"baby boomers," 2
Bach, Johann Sebastian, 52
Barron-Welsh Art Scale, 41
Beauvoir, Simone de, 11, 74, 75
belongingness, 28
Benet, Stephen Vincent, 5
Bernstein, Leonard, 52
black elderly, applied theatre program and, 172, 176
Burger, Isabel, 91
Burgess, Ernest, 7
Butler, Robert, 8

cacoethes studeni ("the itch to learn"), 49
Canal Boats (creative drama exercise), 129-32
Center for Creative Leadership, 51
Center on Arts and Aging, 13
Cervantes, 53
character development, 115, 121-22
Character Lifespan, 101; form, 89
Chayefsky, Paddy, 114

choreopoem-dance, 156-57; adaptation for the hearing impaired, 157
cognitive flexibility, 41, 44
cognitive skills, 14; improved, 14
College Avenue Players, 13
color, physical interpretations, 156
colordance, 156; adaptation for the visually impaired, 156
Comedy of Errors, 73
Coming of Age, The, 11
communication, 153, 158; improved, 14
communication skills, 110
community, sense of, 30
community center, 95
community settings, applied theatre techniques in, 178
companionship, 10
competition, aging and, 38-39
complexity, preference for, 41
concentration, area for, 95
conflict, reaction to, 114
Cranberg, Lawrence, 40
creative capacity, 40
creative drama, 13, 15, 83-105; children and, 87-88; implementation at five sites, 92-100; implementing programs, 91-92; minority elderly, 15; pioneers of, 85-87; with senior adults, 91-92; value of, 86
Creative Dramatics: An Art for Children, 86
Creative Dramatics and English Teaching, 86
Creative Dramatics for the Upper Grades and Junior High School, 86
Creative Dramatics in the Classroom, 86

creative potential, 11-12
creative seniors, examples of, 52-56
creative writing, 16
creativity, 36; age and, 36-47; day-to-day tasks as form of, 55; declines, 39; development of, 88; factors for decline in, 45; five sequential stages of, 51; late life capacities, influence of, 50; measures of, 41; peak periods of, 37; in philosophy and leadership, 50; qualitative and quantitative differences, by age, 42-43; of science and invention, 50; study of, 37-38
Cuffe, Henry, 74
Curie, Marie, 54

dance, integration of in drama exercise, 156
dance-movement activities as applied theatre technique, 153-58
data analysis, 169-73
data collection, 17; qualitative and quantitative, 17
death, issue of, 176, 177
demographic overview, 1-5
De Morgan, William F., 53
Dennis, Wayne, 37
depression, 9; effects of drama program, 159
Differences in the Ages of Mans Life, 74
disengagement theory, 10, 21-25, 176; criticism of, 24-25; most important critique of, 25
divergent thinking, 40-41, 44; risk taking and, 44; testing procedures and, 45

drama, 14; in classrooms, methods for incorporating, 86-87; effects of on elderly, 14. *See also* creative drama
Drama Activities with Older Adults, 66
drama group: audience presence and, 98; general room for, 95; handicapped participants, 146
drama room, 95
dramatic play, with children, 88
Duggar, Benjamin, 54
Durkheim, Emile, 23-27

Edison, Thomas, 54
education: and creative drama, 86; role-playing for, 84
Egyptian theatre, 83
Einstein, Albert, 54
elderly, 1, 13; black, 15 (*see also* black elderly); creative dramatics, 13-14; governing factors, in any society, 8; increase since 1900, 1; loneliness of, 9; negative stereotyping, 8; problems affecting, 6; social reintegration of, 11; as unique individuals, 80; view of, by young, 9. *See also* senior adult
Emma, 136-42; book dramatization, 136-37; preproduction activities, 137
emotions: acting out of, 111; identifying, 151; musical, 151; physical release, 153; release of, 13
environment: aesthetic, 98, 101; age segregated, 177; physical, 98
esteem, loss of, 7
Euripides, 70, 72

experience, sense of, 101
expressive roles, 12

feelings, creative expression of, 176
Fiedler, Arthur, 52
Fill-in-the-Blank Participatory Theatre, 132-35
film, 80; impact of, 81
finances, 8; shrinking, 8
found sounds, 151-52; adaptation for hearing impaired, 152; adaptation for visually impaired, 152
Franck, Cesar Auguste, 52
free verse, 111
Freud, Sigmund, 53
Frost, Robert, 53
frustration, 114
fun, 13
functionalism, 22; leading exponent of, 23
future research, directions for, 176-78

Gallilei, Galileo, 54
Galten, 36
Gandhi, Mahatma, 55
Georgetown, 134
gifted handicapped, 147
Goethe, 53
Grandma Moses, 54
"graying of the United States," 1
Graying of Working America, The, 2
Greek theatre, 83; images of aging, 70-73
group memberships, 29
Group Poem, 91, 101, 156, 157; feelings, 111; free verse, 110; seasonal, 111
group poetry, 16
group skills, 14; improved, 14

Growing Old: The Process of Disengagement, 21
Guilford's tests, 41, 42
Guthrie Theatre, 80, 116

Hagen, Uta, 115
Hals, Franz, 53
handicapped seniors, *see* handicapped elderly
handicapped elderly, 124; applied theatre techniques with, 147-60; working with, 160
haplessness, 9
happiness, U.S. formula for, 25
health, 8; declining, 8
hearing impaired: choreopoem, adaptation for, 157; found sounds, adaptation for, 152; musical characters, adaptation for, 151; musical emotions, adaptation for, 151; musical parts, adaptation for, 150
helplessness, 9
hopelessness, 9
Houle, Cyril, 49
housing satisfaction, 30
human relations, creativity in, 55

identity, loss of, 7
"identity crisis," 6
illiterate seniors, 124
"imagination quotient," 56
immigration, high rates prior to World War II, 1
improvisation, 16
improvisational theatre: plot outline, 112-13; technique, 112-16
Improvisations for the Theatre, 107
independence, 80

individual intuition, importance of, 85
infant mortality, 2; reduction in, 2
instruments, 44; validity of to measure creativity, 43-44
intergenerational learning experience, 122
intergenerational participatory theatre, 128-43; three categories, 128
intergenerational programming, availability of children for, 98
intergenerational relationships, 76
intergenerational theatre, 16
intimate relationship, importance of, 10
intuition, development of, 88
institutionalized retirement, new leisure and, 11
Invitation to the Theatre, 112

Jerome, Judson, 111
job training, role-playing for, 84

Keats, Ezra Jack, 124
Kesselman, Wendy, 136, 137
King Lear, 73, 74, 75
Kozelka, Paul, 13

labor, division of, 23
labor force: female participation rate, 3; male participation in, 3; participants, by age, group, and sex, 3-4
learning-oriented adult learner, 49
Lehman, Harvey C., 36-39
leisure time, 5
life, 2; prolongation of, 2
life cycle development model of creativity, 51
life expectancy, 3, 5
life satisfaction, 30; assessment of, 165; quantitative analyses, 170
lifespan: aesthetic assessment, 89-91; changes, 43; creativity over the, 36-56
listening skills, increasing, 149
literate seniors, 124
literature, introduction and review of, 36-47
living environments, of elderly, 30
Living Stage (Washington, D.C.), 13
"load shedding," 45
loneliness, 7, 9, 17; emotional and social component in, 10; factors contributing to, 9-10; measuring, 166; quantitative analyses, 170; self-perceptions of, 17
longevity, new leisure and, 11
Lysistrata, 70, 72

McCaslin, Nellie, 86
Maggie-Magalita, 137
malapropism, 76
"master status," 7
mathematicians, age and creativity, 54
meaninglessness, sense of, 7
Medea, 70, 72, 77; revival, 77
Meir, Golda, 55
memory, improved, 14
memory function, 123
Michaelangelo, 53
middle-aged children, and their aging parents, 79
Milton, John, 53
minority aged, 15

mirror exercises, 107-10; designated emotion, negative, 109; designated emotion, positive, 109; group focus, 108; silent partner, 109; specific focus, 107-108; undesignated focus, 108; value of, 110
modern theatre, 83
Monet, Claude, 53
Monteverdi, Claudio, 52
morale, effects of age-segregation on, 30
Mother, The, 79, 80, 114
Mother Theresa of Calcutta, 55
movement, 16; development of, 88
music: age and creativity in, 52; as an applied theatre technique, 148-52; integration of in drama exercise, 156
musical characters, 150-51; adaptation for hearing impaired, 151; adaptation for visually impaired, 151
musical emotions, 151; adaptation for hearing impaired, 151; adaptation for visually impaired, 151
musical instruments, objects used as, 151
musical parts, 149-50; adaptation for hearing impaired, 150

National Council on the Aging (NCOA), 13
National Council on the Aging-Arts, 13
National Institute of Mental Health, 46
"new Leisure class," 5, 11-12
nonhandicapped seniors, 124
nonverbal communication, 110
nutrition center, for elderly, 93
nutrition sites, 177

occupational role, loss of, 6
occupational success, 8
old age, 6, 7. *See also* elderly
Older Americans of Stage, 15
older people, *see* elderly
On Golden Pond, 77, 80
Oral History Theatre, 16, 116, 119; advantages of, 116; scenarios developed, 119-23
oral history theatre techniques, 116-23; topics for discussion, 117-18
Orientation to the Theatre, 69

Parsons, Talcott, 23
participatory historical theatre, 128-32
participatory storybook theatre, 135-43
participatory theatre, 93
peace, age and creativity in, 55
peer support, 92
personal imagination, development of, 85
personality, creative, 48
person-centered approach, to study of creativity, 40
physically impaired, scarf-chairdancing, adaptation for, 154
physical movement, encouraging, 149
physical space, assessment of, 92-100
Physics Today, 40
pioneers, of creative drama, 85-87
planned retirement communities, 30; comparative study of, 30-31

playwright's script, power of, 69
playwriting, 143; guidelines, 145
Poet and the Poem, The, 111
politics, age and creativity in, 55
process-centered approach, to study of creativity, 40
production, creative, 40
production-minded, devaluing elderly in, 9
productivity, 36; age and, 36-47; peak of, for different professions, 37-47
productivity peak, 37-47
Prophet, The, 12
Providing Programs for the Gifted Handicapped, 147
psychological well-being, 166
psychometric tests, aging and, 46

qualitative analyses, 171-73
quantitative analyses, 169-71

radio drama script, development of, 124
Rembrandt, 53
Renaissance theatre technique, 112
research, suggestions for, 175-81
restoration drama: audience, 76, 77; imaging of aging, 75-77; innovations in, 75-76
retirees, theatre for, 13
retirement, 4, 7, 10; housing, 29; social loneliness, 10
rhythm-movement master, 154, 156
rhythms: identifying, 150; physical interpretations of, 154

risk-taking, 41, 44; fears, 44, 45
Rivals, The, 76
Roberts, Vera Mowry, 13
"roleless role," 7
role-playing, 84, 158
Rubenstein, Arthur, 52
Rules of Sociological Method, The, 23
Russell, Bertrand, 53

Salk, Jonas, 180
Santayana, 53
Sandburg, Carl, 53
scarf-chairdancing, 153-54; adaptation for physically impaired, 154
scenework, improvisational, as mode for playwriting, 144-46
scientific inventors, age and creativity, 54
scriptwriting, original, 143-44
self, 14, 22; focusing concern, 22; improved sense of, 14
self-actualized individual, 49
self-concept, 7, 9, 79; positive, 92; reaffirming, 27
self-confidence, establishing, 101
self-esteem, 9; improved sense of, 14
self-exploration, 13
self-expression, 153
self-identification, 166
self-pacing, 45
self-teacher, 48
senior adults: actor training techniques, 106-107; awareness of experiences and talents, 101; character lifespan assessment, 89-90; creative drama and, 66, 91; dance-movement activities, 153-58;

improvisational theatre, 112; theatre programs, 80; utilization of self, 115-16; visual arts activities, 157-58
"senior-boom," 2
sensory recall, 115, 122
Shakespeare, William, image of aging, 73-75
Shaw Test, 41
Sheldon, Edward Austin, 86
She Stoops to Conquer, 76
"significant others," 7, 27
Siks, Geraldine Brain, 85, 86
Slade, Peter, 88
social groups, 26; personal involvement in, 26, 28
social integration, 6, 7, 11, 27-32; decrease in, 6
social interaction, 10, 22; widow-hood, 10; withdrawal from, 22
social isolation, 10
socialization, 14, 29; concomitant, 29; improved, 14
social roles, 7, 8, 29; loss of, 7, 8
social values, 29
society, reintegration of elderly in, 11
sociodrama, 158; as applied theatre technique, 158-60; defined, 158; problems, 159; role-playing, 158
Sophocles, 53
sound effects, producing, 128
specific event, story centering on, 128
Spolin, Viola, 107
status, loss of, 7
stereotyping, 8; negative, 8, 9
structure-of-intellectual model, 40
study design, applied theatre techniques: demographic characteristics of study participants, 164; dependent variables, 165; subjects, 163-65
subjective age identification, 166; change in, 170
suicide, 9, 10, 28; age group, 10; high rates, 28
symbolic interaction, 26; theories of, 26-27
symbolic interactionists, 26

talking book project, children as audience members, 128
Talking Book Series, 16, 123-28; advantages, 123-24
Tate, Ruth, 13
technology, new leisure and, 11
television, 80
tension, release of, 176
tests: reliability of, 45; validity of, 43-44
theatre groups, senior adult, 66
Theatre of Feast, 80
theatre programs, senior adult, 80
theatre techniques with elderly, 106; improvisational, 112-16; intergenerational participatory theatre, 128-43; mirror exercises, 107-112; oral history theatre, 116-23; Talking Book Series, 123-28
theoretical/conceptual models, on creativity and aging, 47-51
theoretical implications, applied theatre program, 176-78
therapeutic art, 147
Third Age Theatre, 13
Tintoretto, 53
Titian, 53
Tolstoy, L., 53

Torrance's test of creative thinking, 41

Ulyssean adults, 48-49, 52; description of, 49
uneasiness, 7
United States, contemporary drama in, 77

Van Bennder, Pierre Joseph, 54
verbal communication, 110; understanding, 123
verbal skills, improved, 14
Verdi, Guiseppe, 52
visual aids, 118
visual and audio arts activities, 93
visual arts, 16, 124, 157; as applied theatre technique, 157-58; integration of in drama exercise, 156
visually impaired: colordance, adaptation for, 156; found sounds, adaptation for, 152; musical emotions, adaptation for, 151

vocal patterns, understanding, 123
von Humboldt, Friedrich Heinrich, 54

Ward, Winifred, 86
Way, Brian, 85
Whistle for Willie, 124
Who, What, Where Improvisation, 113, 120, 159; character focus, 114; personal experience, 114; stuck in, 113
widowhood, 6, 7
wisdom, as quality of old, 56
Woodworth, Robert S., 36
work, productive, 3
Wright, Frank Lloyd, 54
writers, famous, creativity and age and, 53

Yeats, William Butler, 53
youth-oriented, devaluing elderly in, 9

ABOUT THE AUTHORS

PATCH CLARK currently serves as an advisor to Very Special Arts-Virginia. She has served as a Creative Arts Consultant to nursing homes, public and private schools, retirement centers, and nutrition sites. She has taught acting, creative drama, and applied theatre studies for handicapped and senior adults at Virginia Commonwealth University in Richmond, Virginia. She holds A.A., B.F.A., and M.F.A. degrees in Theatre, Performance, and Theatre Education. Her latest radio play, *Same Blue Eyes*, was selected for production by WBKY-FM and Donovan Little Theatre-Council on Aging, University of Kentucky, during the academic year 1983-1984.

NANCY J. OSGOOD is Assistant Professor of Gerontology and Sociology at Virginia Commonwealth University/Medical College of Virginia in Richmond. A former member of the National Committee on Vital and Health Statistics, Dr. Osgood has interests that include health and mental health of the aged. She has published and presented several papers on the topics of creative dramatics for the elderly and recreation, leisure and aging. Dr. Osgood just organized and chaired a session entitled "Creative Arts and Aging" for the National Recreation and Park Association annual meetings. Her other interests center around retirement and retirement preparation, housing and environments, and suicide among the elderly. Dr. Osgood recently completed *Life After Work: Retirement, Leisure, Recreation, and the Elderly* and *Senior Settlers: Social Integration in Retirement Communities*, both published by Praeger Publishers and *Suicide in the Elderly: A Practitioner's Guide to Diagnosis and Mental Health Intervention* published by Aspen Systems Corporation. Dr. Osgood teaches classes in social gerontology, recreation, leisure, and aging, community and community services for the aged. Her Ph.D. in sociology and certificate in gerontology were earned at Syracuse University in 1979.